TOWARDS MORE EFFECTIVE OPEN AND DISTANCE TEACHING

I have much pleasure in dedicating this book to my wife, Delma, a loving and supportive marriage partner and friend for close on 30 years.

TOWARDS MORE EFFECTIVE OPEN AND DISTANCE TEACHING

Perc Marland

KOGAN PAGE

London • Stirling (USA)

Published in association with the
Institute of Educational Technology, Open University

First published in 1997

Apart from any fair dealing for the purposes of research or private study, or criticism or review, as permitted under the Copyright, Designs and Patents Act, 1988, this publication may only be reproduced, stored or transmitted, in any form or by any means, with the prior permission in writing of the publishers, or in the case of reprographic reproduction in accordance with the terms of licences issued by the Copyright Licensing Agency. Enquiries concerning reproduction outside those terms should be sent to the publishers at the undermentioned address:

Kogan Page Limited
120 Pentonville Road
London N1 9JN
and
22883 Quicksilver Drive
Stirling, VA 20166, USA

© Perc Marland, 1997

British Library Cataloguing in Publication Data

A CIP record for this book is available from the British Library.

ISBN 0 7494 2190 8 paperback
ISBN 0 7494 2189 4 hardback

Typeset by JS Typesetting, Wellingborough, Northants.
Printed and bound in Great Britain by
Biddles Ltd, Guildford and King's Lynn

Contents

Series editor's foreword ... vii

1. **Personal Practical Theories: Keys to Effective Teaching** ... 1
   Focus of chapter ... 1
   Scientific knowledge and practical know-how ... 2
   Practical knowledge ... 4
   Practical theory ... 6
   Teachers' practical theories ... 7
   Articulation of practical theories ... 11
   Summary ... 14

2. **Teachers' Practical Theories: Substance and Structure** ... 15
   Review ... 15
   Focus of chapter ... 16
   Substance of teachers' practical theories ... 17
   Structure of teachers' practical theories ... 39
   Other ways of categorizing teachers' knowledge ... 42
   The practical theory of a distance teacher – an example ... 44
   Summary ... 49

3. **Practical Theories of Teaching: Review and Revision** ... 51
   Review ... 51
   Focus of chapter ... 51
   Introduction ... 52
   Reflection ... 53
   Journal writing ... 60
   Use of metaphors ... 61
   Action research ... 63
   Conclusion ... 65

4. **Review and Revision of Practical Theories of Distance Teaching: Some Issues for Consideration**   67
   Review   67
   Focus of chapter   68
   Issue 1: Open learning in distance education   68
   Implications of open learning for practical theories of distance teaching   72
   Issue 2: Knowledge of students   76
   Extending knowledge of individual students: implications for practical theories of distance teaching   82
   Issue 3: Student interactivity   84
   Extending student interactivity: implications for practical theories of distance teaching   87

5. **Review and Revision of Practical Theories of Distance Teaching: Additional Issues**   93
   Focus of chapter   93
   Issue 4: Promoting better learning   94
   An approach to facilitating deep learning: implications for practical theories of distance teaching   106
   Issue 5: Facilitating student access to the content of distance materials   107
   Implications of access devices for practical theories of distance teaching   110
   Concluding remarks   112

References   113

Author Index   121

Subject Index   125

Series editor's foreword

The publication of this book could not have come at a better time, nor could it present a more important challenge. It is published at a time when there is dramatic growth in open and distance learning around the world and when an increasing number of colleagues are being asked to teach via these methods. It is published at a time when all of us are being encouraged to improve the quality of our students' learning. The challenge Perc Marland makes is for us to identify the basis of our teaching practices and assess their likely influence on resultant teaching quality and student learning; the evidence presented reveals there is much room for improvement.

In *Towards More Effective Open and Distance Teaching*, Marland argues that our teaching practices are based on our personal, practical theories of teaching; theories that are often implied, influential but seldom articulated. He provides arguments for recognizing the value of our personal experiences in teaching, reflecting on them and revising our teaching accordingly. During the initial part of the book Marland reviews the evidence and lists those components of the practical theories of teachers he believes can influence our practice – Values, beliefs and goals; Student states and cues; Strategies, tactics and techniques; Principles; Teacher attributes; Contextual factors; Metaphors and images; and Pedagogical content knowledge. In reviewing their importance he draws on research in both schools and higher education. Later in the book he discusses the work of Schön and the concept of the reflective practitioner and how this can be utilized; his explanation of ways to become more reflective is one of the clearest you will find. The final part of the book addresses probably the most important task facing us today – how to promote student learning. After reviewing the evidence, and accepting the dynamic process of utilizing the most appropriate approach to study in relation to perceived demands, Marland focuses on the benefits of deep approaches to learning. He outlines a way to facilitate a deep approach and explains how the teacher, in the role of 'cognitive coach', can facilitate it.

A major feature of this book are the numerous 'Invitations to Reflect'. These provide probing questions designed to help us reconsider our practical theories of teaching and opportunities to revise our teaching. It is clear that as teachers we are able to improve our teaching if we are prepared to review and revise our practical theories of teaching. Indeed, as I read this book I found myself returning to the phrase 'tell me it's difficult, tell me it's time consuming, but don't tell me you can't do it'.

This book represents a major contribution to raising our awareness of teachers practical theories – how they can be reviewed and revised – and how they can contribute to improved teaching.

Fred Lockwood

Chapter 1

Personal practical theories: keys to effective teaching

Focus of Chapter

Success in many domestic, work and leisure related activities depends on possessing the appropriate know-how. This applies to simple activities such as operating a tin opener or threading a needle, as well as to complex activities such as sailing a yacht, tuning the engine of a modern car or solving problems at work. The know-how required for these activities is often largely the product of experience and, because it has been acquired from on-the-job learning rather than through formal education, remains tacit and difficult to articulate. Even where scientific or formal knowledge has much to offer the practitioner, experientially based skill still plays a key part. The importance of this practical know-how is often overlooked.

This chapter will explore the nature and significance of know-how derived from practical activity and will argue that awareness and refinement by distance teachers of their practical know-how is the key to improving the effectiveness of open and distance teaching.

Three basic propositions are examined in relation to teaching:

1. that what each of us does as a learner or teacher is shaped in powerful ways by a kind of know-how which is largely implicit and difficult to articulate;

2. that this know-how is grounded largely in our own experiences as teachers but also as learners; and
3. that, to improve our effectiveness as teachers, we need critically to review and revise the know-how that underpins our performance in this role.

The essential prerequisite to a review of what shapes our teaching and how to improve it is that we are fully conversant with all aspects of our practical know-how. Because parts of our practical know-how are implicit, the task of explicating them presents a challenge. This challenge and ways of responding to it are explored towards the end of the chapter.

Scientific Knowledge and Practical Know-how

Significance of scientific knowledge

For most of this century, we have been encouraged to place considerable faith in the power of scientific knowledge. This kind of knowledge, we have been told, can make a significant contribution to solving many of society's problems and improving our quality of life. By and large, that faith has not been misplaced as advances in such fields as transport, medicine, telecommunications and agriculture attest. We only have to cast our minds back a couple of decades to the era of slow-speed dental drills, ink-based devices for copying, mechanical typewriters and pre-satellite means of communication to find other reminders of the benefits of scientific endeavour.

Another kind of knowledge

However, this faith in scientific knowledge has blinded us somewhat to the power of other kinds of knowledge. In fact, many aspects of our daily lives are shaped, and in most instances quite effectively, by our drawing on a largely tacit knowledge which derives from personal experience. This private know-how is built up, sometimes without much apparent mental effort on our part, from our attempts to make sense of the situations we encounter and the activities in which we engage. In short, this tacit knowledge is a product of learning from experience. The knowledge we accumulate this way, which is acquired through a thoughtful process of trial and error, is gradually refined until it provides a reliable and serviceable basis for action, or until events unfold which challenge its worth. Then, if it no longer serves us well, we look for a substitute. Two examples of this experience-based knowledge and its powerful place in our lives are provided below.

Examples
The first example concerns the legendary sailing skills of South Sea Islanders. Long before the benefits of satellite technology and other modern scientific

navigational devices were available, these people were able to find their way across vast expanses of the Pacific Ocean from one tiny island cluster to another. How were they able to accomplish these amazing feats? Morris West provides some insights in *The Navigators*. West reminds us that the amazing navigational skills of South Sea Islanders were based on a knowledge accumulated over generations from actual sailing experience. They found their way across the virtually featureless, watery plains of the Pacific by using a variety of signs, all built up from hard-won experience – the flight paths of migrating birds, evidence in cloud formations of updrafts caused by land, the presence of driftwood and seaweed, deviations in currents caused by islands and reflections in clouds of the green lagoons surrounding islands.

The second example comes from industry and was related by to me a metallurgist friend who had been employed at a steel mill in his youth. Quality checks of the finished product at the mill had disclosed, over a short period of time, a serious decline in the quality of the steel being produced. The cause was eventually traced to a staff change. At that time, responsibility for the production process had passed from an old experienced operator to a new and relatively inexperienced employee. Checks showed that both apparently adhered to the same formulae and processes. However, after lengthy investigation, which involved recall of the retired expert and careful probing of his knowledge and procedures, it was found that the difference in production quality lay in the ability of the old hand to make subtle adjustments during the production process. These adjustments were based on the expert's careful search for critical signs in the process of converting ore into steel, knowing what those signs meant and knowing what action to take when they appeared.

In the first example, the know-how appears to have been derived from actual sailing experience, with observation and trial and error presumably playing an important part in its development. The knowledge gained from this experience was gradually accumulated and passed on to younger members of the culture and incorporated into the knowledge and folkways of the society. In the second example, the expert mill operator had improved the steel manufacturing process by blending a knowledge of formulae and processes, grounded in scientific research, with a knowledge gained from years of experience and on-the-job learning.

There are many other everyday examples of the significance of experiential knowledge. Parenting experiences, for example, provide a principal source of the knowledge that parents use to understand the behaviours of their children and to find better ways of interacting with, and disciplining, them and promoting their welfare. Some parents would admit that their knowledge of parenting owed little to textbooks or parent preparation courses. Other parents may have started out with some knowledge from classes on parenting or from materials they had read. At the same time, most parents would acknowledge that there was a steady improvement, after their first child, in the quality of their parenting practices – improvements they would attribute to experience.

Experience also provides real estate agents with knowledge about the best ways of relating to clients and conducting themselves in the presence of sellers and buyers. Experience also provides opportunities for refining knowledge gained initially from formal courses. Such knowledge is an important ingredient in a successful real estate career. Cricketers, through sometimes painful experiences, acquire knowledge about variations in the flight and bounce of cricket balls on variable surfaces and in different climatic conditions. This knowledge forms a core part of the mental equipment of successful cricketers and has been used to formulate or refine techniques in bowling and batting. It has sometimes even been referred to as theory – cricket experts often allude to theories of swing bowling. In fact, in most sports, raw talent is an important but insufficient ingredient, but experience is also required before it can be fully realized.

Practical Knowledge

The kind of knowledge illustrated above has been variously titled working knowledge (Yinger *et al.*, 1991), craft knowledge (Brown and McIntyre, 1988), and tacit knowledge (Schön, 1983). It has also been referred to as practical knowledge (Elbaz, 1983) which is the term that will be used throughout this text. Practical knowledge, then, is knowledge which is used to get things done in practical situations. As the above illustrations indicate, practical knowledge can be derived in at least two ways – from experience and thoughtful reflection on that experience; and from experience involving the thoughtful use of scientific knowledge in practical situations. In the metallurgy case, for example, practical experience with scientific knowledge in the production of minerals from ore has apparently resulted in some modification of scientific knowledge to produce a more potent and useful form of this knowledge. This new form of knowledge is still, in part, the product of experience and, though it owes much to science and research, has been appropriated and modified, in this case, by a metallurgist as a result of experience. For these reasons, and because it is used in a practical situation, it is not inappropriate to refer to this modified version of scientific knowledge as practical knowledge.

This example illustrates the close links that can exist between practical knowledge and scientific knowledge and, for that matter, other forms of knowledge. Scientific knowledge can be used to inform our practical tasks, and then adapted over time to suit the particular circumstances that arise there. On the other hand, if practices are already in place, scientific knowledge can be used to study and improve what we do and the know-how on which our practice is based. This, according to Brookfield (1995), is the case in education. He makes the point that educational literature, which contains formal theory and findings from research, 'can help us investigate the hunches, instincts, and tacit knowledge that shape our practice. It can suggest different possibilities for practice, as well as helping us understand better what we already do and think' (p.185). The industry example also reflects a changed view of the place of research knowledge in contemporary professional practice. As Donmoyer (1996) notes, 'Today, knowledge is more likely to be seen as a heuristic to guide practice rather than as a source of formulas that dictate what professionals are to do' (p.98).

Experience, then, is not just the source of a supplementary or trivial type of know-how. Frequently, it is a principal or primary source of the knowledge that informs action. This is certainly so in many non-technological areas, such as those requiring extensive human interaction, where quality work practice simply cannot be reduced to the application of standardized scientific principles and generalizations. Education is a case in point. As Donmoyer (1996) points out, 'there is a general distrust of systems and standard operating procedures as solutions to educational problems' (p.98). This is because education is not a technical enterprise. Educators need to be able to respond flexibly, skilfully and professionally to the idiosyncratic needs of particular learners in particular classrooms. Applying standard recipes to all students in all contexts simply does not work. While teachers may appreciate generalizations from research, they frequently look to the lessons they have learnt from experience as guides for action.

Characteristics of practical knowledge

As we have seen, practical knowledge is the knowledge that is derived from, or shaped by, practice. It is not an automatic product of practice but usually requires that practice be accompanied by some kind of reflection on practice. Practical knowledge is also knowledge that is personally acquired by the individual practitioner and is therefore specific to that person and highly idiosyncratic. It may be of interest and relevance to other practitioners but would not necessarily be personally meaningful to them and could not be appropriated by them for their use without interpretation, modification and some practical trial. One person's practical knowledge is not a commodity which can be universally applied by others performing the same task. This is because it has been crafted by the individual to suit the individual and his or her particular circumstances.

It is also knowledge that has close ties with the particular context or contexts in which the practice occurred. It has been constructed *in* a particular context and *for* that particular context. Practical knowledge, therefore, is said to be situationally bound or context-specific. This means that it cannot be readily used, without some modification, even by the holder, in other contexts. It therefore lacks generalizability across contexts and certainly across different users. However, in the mind of the holder of the knowledge, what it lacks in generalizability it makes up for in terms of potency and validity.

Another characteristic of practical knowledge is that it is tacit or implicit. In other words, it resides mainly in the minds of practitioners and is seldom articulated or set down in print form. This is largely because, until recently, the value of practical knowledge, vis-à-vis scientific knowledge, had largely been overlooked or underestimated. Now that the worth and significance of this wisdom of practice have been widely recognized, attempts have been made to document it but, as we will see later, the explication of this knowledge is difficult.

The last characteristic of practical knowledge to be discussed here is its practicality. Among practitioners, practical knowledge is prized because it is practical – it works and, in the case of expert practitioners, it works very well. Usually, the better the practical knowledge, the better the practice which the knowledge informs. At the same time, it would be wrong to imply that practical knowledge is flawless or even anywhere near perfect. Even the practical knowledge of expert practitioners has its limitations.

Practical Theory

In some work situations involving low-level or simple tasks, the practical knowledge that is applied may be limited in scope, somewhat superficial and fragmented rather than coherent. In other situations, including professional ones, the practical knowledge in use may be quite extensive, complex and integrated and may exhibit a degree of internal consistency. As such, it may provide more than just guidelines or a recipe for the competent completion of a task. It may also provide a basis for understanding events, predicting what is likely to happen and planning appropriate action. In these instances, the body of practical knowledge fulfils some of the functions of theory and is, in fact, referred to as theory.

The theorizing tendency

The use of the term 'theory' to refer to the practical know-how of some practitioners, even those in professional service, might be considered somewhat pretentious, if theorizing is seen as the province only of scientists and researchers. But in fact theorizing can be viewed as a basic aspect of human behaviour. As Kaplan (1964) reminds us,

> a theory is a way of making sense of a disturbing situation (or novel experience) so as to allow us most effectively to bring to bear our repertoire of habits, and even more important, to modify habits or discard them altogether, replacing them by new ones as the situation demands....To engage in theorising means not just to learn by experience but to take thought about what is there to be learned (p.295).

Earlier, a similar view was expressed by Kelly (1955) who proposed that human beings are actively involved in attempting to make sense of the physical and social worlds they inhabit and thereby construct their own versions of the realities they experience. He saw humans as 'personal scientists' who classify and categorize their experiences and theorize about them in order to predict and shape the events in which they participate and their own parts in those events.

This basic tendency in humans to theorize is an everyday occurrence. 'Like it or not', says Brookfield (1995), 'we are all theorists and we are all practitioners' (p.185). We display this tendency to theorize when we seek to understand the behaviour of a friend or colleague, especially when that behaviour is somewhat unusual or troubling to us. We do it when we are playing cards or tennis and want to win, or when we are concerned about our parenting practices and want to improve them. This theorizing tendency also contributed to the acquisition of practical knowledge and practical theory in the instances referred to earlier in this chapter.

Teachers' Practical Theories

Recognition and acceptance of this theorizing tendency in humans has been partly responsible for the popularization, over the last two decades, of the notion of teachers as theory builders and hence the notion of teachers' practical theories (Brown and McIntyre, 1993; Handal and Lauvas, 1987; Sanders and McCutcheon, 1986). Anyone involved in the teaching enterprise, according to Carr and Kemmis (1983), must possess a theory because it is this which provides an understanding of the contexts they are operating in and some notion of the purposes to be served by their work. Moreover, their practical theories shape their decisions and actions. It is now widely accepted that what teachers do is shaped by their own practical theories of teaching. Their theories have been forming throughout their lives but especially during their professional lives, and also during the 13 or so years spent as learners in schools.

Of course, these theories show considerable variation in scope, complexity and usefulness. As might be expected, the practical theories of student teachers, in the early years of their teacher education at least, are often simple, naive and not very serviceable. This is because the classroom experiences from which their practical theories have been derived are limited to those they have had as students. As a result, their theories have not been reality-tested in the classroom and refined by careful reflection or by new perspectives from teacher preparation courses. On the other hand, the practical theories of experienced and effective teachers are prized for their usefulness and feature much higher levels of complexity and sophistication.

A definition of practical theory

Practical theories of teaching are defined by Sanders and McCutcheon (1986) as:

> the conceptual structures and visions that provide teachers with reasons for acting as they do, and for choosing the teaching activities and curriculum materials they choose in order to be effective. They are the principles or propositions that undergird and guide teachers' appreciations, decisions and actions. (pp.54–5)

Further insight into the meaning of the term 'practical theory' is provided by Handal and Lauvas (1987) who use the term in reference to 'a person's private, integrated but ever-changing system of knowledge, experience and values which is relevant to teaching practice at any particular time' (p.9).

Practical theories of teaching and practical knowledge share the same general characteristics outlined earlier. Practical theories are personal, having been constructed by each individual teacher. They are situation-specific, having been designed to suit a particular group of students in a particular classroom. They are usually partly implicit because teachers may be unable to articulate or recall the origins or rationales of their teaching actions. They are intensely practical because they have been synthesized from what works in practice though, as we noted earlier, parts of the knowledge may have come from research or theory.

Practical theories vis-à-vis scientific theories

Practical theories, however, are not regarded as scientific theories because, as Sanders and McCutcheon (1986) have noted, they lack some of the characteristics traditionally associated with scientific theories. For example, they lack conceptual precision, specification in a formal language and generalizability. Moreover, they cannot be subjected to the same rigorous logical tests as scientific theories. Neither have they been formulated for the purpose of establishing a public knowledge base to which others have right of access.

Nevertheless, they do serve some of the functions of theories noted earlier (Marland, 1995). They allow teachers to identify and understand significant elements of the teaching-learning enterprise and the relationships among them. They provide teachers with a capacity to predict what may happen and what may work well. Accordingly, they also provide a sound basis for action in the classroom. For instance, teachers generally 'know' what approach works best with a particular group of students, how best to respond in certain circumstances, which students to involve at a particular instant, what resources to use, what problems students usually encounter, which examples or illustrations really assist student understanding, how best to sequence a lesson, and so on. Thus practical theories allow teachers to understand and explain the contexts in which they work and to predict the course of events and outcomes, all of which are functions of theories.

Significance of teachers' practical theories

The question you might well be asking yourself at this point is: why all the fuss about teachers' practical theories? Some clues have already appeared earlier, but, in case they have escaped your attention, let me gather them all together now. Teachers' practical theories are very important because:

- They provide a basis for what teachers do professionally. The actions of teachers in classrooms, schools and distance education contexts are shaped largely by their own practical theories of teaching.
- They determine teachers' levels of effectiveness. Quality of teaching is, in large measure, a direct function of the quality of the practical theories held by

teachers. Thus improvements in teaching depend on a capacity and willingness to improve one's practical theory.
- They determine the fate of educational innovations and reforms because innovation and reform agendas are all mediated through the minds of teachers. Changes can only find expression in classrooms if teachers are convinced that the changes are worthwhile and are prepared to make adjustments to their practical theories to accommodate those changes. Even then, the changes are not necessarily implemented in the form in which they were proposed. They are selectively adjusted and transformed in accordance with the perspectives of individual teachers. In other words, proposed changes are 'domesticated' to suit the values, beliefs and contexts of the user.

Recognition of the existence and importance of the notion of teachers' practical theories has had reverberations in many areas (Marland, 1995). It has brought into prominence the role of learning from experience and on-the-job learning. It has accorded a new status to practical knowledge and practical theories. It has placed the teacher 'in the driving seat' in relation to curriculum reform (Connelly and Clandinin, 1988). It has required a reformulation of questions in research on teaching and added impetus to a redefinition of the teacher's role in research. It has prompted major change to views on the professional development of teachers and to pre-service teacher education (Marland, 1993). In fact, there has been so much interest in the practical theories of teachers and so much significance attached to them that the study of teachers' practical theories has been a dominant field of research inquiry for most of the last decade (Clark, 1988).

Implications for teachers in classrooms

As the foregoing makes clear, the concepts of teachers' practical knowledge and theories now hold a place of prominence in the world of education and research in teaching, one which they did not previously enjoy. Only in the last two decades has experientially derived or experientially modified knowledge been recognized as significant in teaching. Prior to that, the only knowledge considered to be of value to teachers was that produced by researchers (Feiman-Nemser and Floden, 1986).

The prestige and significance now attached to practical knowledge and theories place important responsibilities on teachers. Teachers must now assume responsibility for getting to know and understand fully what it is that shapes their professional actions. They must be able to account and provide a valid rationale for their actions. This responsibility will involve them in making explicit their own practical theories, theories which, as we have seen, have, in part at least, remained implicit even to the holder. A second major responsibility is that they must take an active role in their own professional development by reflecting on, and seeking to provide justification for, their own practical theories and, where necessary, reviewing, revising and updating them. These are individual responsibilities for each and every teacher because practical theories have to be crafted by individuals to suit the personal attributes of each teacher and the specific contexts in which that teacher works. These are crucial professional obligations that can not be devolved to others.

What acceptance of the notion of teachers' practical theories also requires is that teaching not be assessed for quality by examining only teaching processes and learning outcomes. Such an approach is not acceptable since it takes, as unproblematic, the orientation or philosophy from which the teaching processes and learning outcomes stemmed. No one, for example, would be satisfied with a competent, even exemplary, use of explicit teaching or direct instructional techniques in a lesson if it was known that the goal of the lesson was to foster creativity. Means must be evaluated by reference to ends or purposes and these must be morally and educationally defensible. Similarly, no one would condone an approach to teaching which breached ethical principles even if it produced highly satisfactory results. For example, the use of fear and violence in classrooms to secure high levels of student performance would simply not be tolerated. It is essential, therefore, that teachers scrutinize critically the beliefs, values, principles, assumptions, goals and knowledge bases in which their teaching is grounded as well as what they do (processes) and what is achieved (outcomes). In short, their obligation to their students, society and themselves is to subject their practical theories to continuous and critical scrutiny.

These basic responsibilities and obligations apply to all teachers, but it is especially important in the case of novice teachers or those without an adequate preparation for the teaching role. This latter situation sometimes arises in universities where academic staff appointments are usually made on the basis of criteria relating to research expertise or potential but where teaching qualifications or experience receive scant attention. Where teachers lack both wisdom from practice and knowledge from professional studies in education, the quality of teaching can be under serious threat. Quality in education is unlikely to be achieved where, for example, teachers lack the knowledge to be able to make appropriate assumptions about learners, to match educational means to educational goals and to adopt sound principles for the evaluation of student learning. In those circumstances, practice is based only on naive theories about teaching which are derived from vague and piecemeal notions about what it means to teach, notions which have not been subjected to critical examination.

Implications for those who teach distance learners

The responsibilities referred to above are common to all teachers, including those involved with distance learners. It is important that distance educators also explicate their practical theories of distance education because, once again, their theories give rise to their actions. Practical theories will influence the actions the distance teachers take on such important matters as the nature of the materials they prepare, the form and frequency of their contacts with learners and contacts they promote among learners, the systems they develop to support distance learners and the ways they open up education to maximize student choice. If there is no awareness by distance teachers of the grounds for their actions, there is little likelihood that the underlying theories can be critically assessed and the theories and the actions to which they give rise improved. What remains outside conscious awareness cannot receive due attention in self-evaluation.

In keeping with the model provided above, the second responsibility of distance teachers is to ensure that a critical eye is cast over their practical theories to determine how and where they can be improved and extended. Fulfilling this responsibility is no simple matter for any distance teacher (ways of doing so will become the focus of later chapters) but, for some, it is very challenging. It is especially difficult for those who become distance teachers without any formal preparation for the role and who have not had experience as distance learners themselves. They are then ill-prepared for the role of distance teacher. They lack a robust and serviceable practical theory. Even their intuitive notions about what distance teaching involves are probably poorly informed. One could speculate that their intuitions and hunches might derive from experience gained from reading novels, studying textual material and listening to television broadcasts. Although helpful, these experiences do not provide an adequate basis for the design of distance materials. Additionally or alternately, they might be dependent on insights gained vicariously from others engaged in distance studies. In these circumstances, their practical theories about distance teaching would very likely be inadequate. Of course, their problems are exacerbated if institutional or collegial support is lacking.

Reviewing teaching via practical theories, therefore, has two significant advantages. One is that the tacit or more obscure reasons for teaching the way we do are made explicit and can be exposed to critical assessment. Thus, those aspects of our approaches to teaching which were routinized early in our careers or which are based on time-honoured customs and folk-ways that were accepted unquestioningly are more likely to receive critical scrutiny. The second is that practical theories offer an holistic and integrated or coherent view of teaching. They remind us that teaching is organic, that all the components are intertwined. Just as good medical practice requires that patient care involve consideration of the whole person, not just treatment of an ailment or injury, so caring for the way one teaches requires attention to the whole of one's approach to teaching, as represented by the practical theory, not just a part of it. Using practical theories as a reference point in reflections on teaching, therefore, is more likely to discourage our inclination to excise one small part of our teaching theory and practice for close examination and ignore other related parts.

Articulation of Practical Theories

If teachers are to examine and revise their practical theories in order to enhance their effectiveness, they need first to articulate them. Doing so is no simple task. It requires teachers to introspect or look into their own minds in an attempt to make explicit the rationale for their teaching behaviour. Some of the techniques which can help teachers to articulate their own practical theories are outlined below. In addition, teachers wishing to become aware of their own practical theories may derive some benefit from knowing about the scope and structure of practical theories and the constructs used in their documentation. This material is reviewed in Chapter 2. In addition, activities have been built into the text to assist readers in the articulation process, but now let us return to an examination of ways of articulating practical theories or assisting their articulation. Some of the difficulties will also be considered.

Articulation difficulties

Difficulty in explicating practical theories stems from two main factors. One is that parts of a teachers' practical theory may be implicit. It is possible that some of these parts had their origins in the early life experiences of the teacher and therefore fall into the realm of the taken-for-granted, having been formed intuitively or adopted uncritically and without reference to the culture of teaching. Other parts may have become implicit because they have been routinized, with teachers no longer aware of the bases for their actions. They may find that it is not necessary even to think about what they are going to do before doing it. The other factor is that teachers have not had much practice in articulating their practical theories. Opportunities to do so have been restricted because, until recently, little heed has been paid to what teachers know and, as a result, they are largely unskilled in the art. Thus, it is not easy for teachers to document their practical theories. It is not just a matter of unzipping teachers' minds to reveal the contents. Making practical theories explicit will require a long and careful search of memory, the reconstruction of past experience and reflection on the roots of practice, and will involve not a little self-discovery.

Articulation – ways and means

Finding ways of assisting teachers to disclose their practical theories has been exercising the minds of researchers for quite some time. As Calderhead (1996) has noted, 'Methods of eliciting the knowledge, beliefs, and thinking of teachers have frequently been borrowed from the fields of cognitive psychology, human problem solving, social anthropology, and the humanities' (p.711). He describes these methods under five categories – simulations, commentaries, concept mapping and repertory grid, ethnography and case studies, and narratives. Much of this work has proceeded on the assumption that details of practical theories can be made known through teacher discourse and through their actions, since actions are overt expressions of their covert theories. Not surprisingly, then, techniques for assisting the explication of practical theories have included interviews, participant observation, journal keeping and seeking teacher commentary on video and audio records of teaching. All these methods yield verbal data which contain or denote the form and substance of the practical theories of teachers. Other frequently used methods include the life history method (But *et al.*, 1988; Woods, 1987) and the repertory grid technique (Yaxley, 1991). Often these methods involve researchers as assistants in the disclosure process.

Where teachers wishing to fully articulate their own practical theories are not in partnership with researchers, there will probably need to be a greater emphasis on self-inquiry. In this situation, a teacher can engage in an internal dialogue, a conversation with him or herself. This process might begin with an account of what they do as teachers and identification of patterns and principles underlying their practices. This could then lead to a phase of prolonged self-interrogation about the reasons and bases for their actions. Of course, there are many ways of assisting this self-disclosure process. Teachers can keep journals of events in their classrooms and use these to explore the reasons for their actions. They can engage in discussions about their teaching with their colleagues or could use their colleagues, first as observers to record events, and then as critical friends (Francis, 1995) to assist in uncovering the underlying theory. This would be relatively simple to arrange where teachers are in teaching teams and regularly observe each other teaching.

In brief then, the two basic steps in becoming aware of your own practical theory or 'what makes you tick' as a teacher, are: (1) description; and (2) analysis. Description involves, *inter alia*:

- Outlining what you do as a teacher by referring to the strategies, behaviours, ways of responding, ways of projecting self, interactions with students and anything else that is descriptive of you in the teaching role. Aids to this process include journal-keeping, audio-visual records and seeking from observers descriptive accounts of what you do.
- Preparing a brief biographical sketch of your life, including events or experiences which have had an important influence on what you do, believe, and value.

Analysis involves identifying why you do what you do as a teacher through, *inter alia*:

- Self-interrogation.
- Discussions with colleagues.
- Searching for answers through your personal and professional past.

Summary

The chapter began with a brief exploration of the nature of practical know-how. Practical know-how was described as knowledge that is particularly useful for getting practical things done. It was seen also as a product of practical experience and reflection on that experience. Some characteristics of practical knowledge were also noted, including its implicitness and the fact that it is highly contextualized and individualistic or person-specific. Where this practical know-how is extensive, complex and interrelated, and provides a consistent and reliable basis for understanding and explaining practical activities and the associated phenomena, and for predicting events and deciding appropriate action, it has been referred to as practical theory.

Some time was spent pointing out the importance of practical theories, especially in the field of teaching and, in particular, distance teaching. It has been proposed that a key to improving the quality of teaching lies in becoming aware of what it is that shapes our behaviours as teachers, namely our practical theories, subjecting these to careful and sustained scrutiny and changing them where this appears warranted. The chapter concluded with a brief look at ways of articulating practical theories and the difficulties involved.

Chapter 2

Teachers' practical theories: substance and structure

Review A number of fundamental premises about teaching and how to improve teaching were outlined in the first chapter. The first was that what we do as teachers is shaped by our own personal practical theories of teaching. The second was that, in order to improve our teaching, we must effect changes to our practical theories or the fundamental reasons we have for teaching the way we do. Acceptance of this last premise requires that we be very clear about the content and structure of our practical theories. This is necessary so that we can understand fully the bases for our actions and determine what changes need to be made to our theories to improve our performance.

There is nothing very novel about these two premises. They are applied every day in some areas of human activity and with varying degrees of success. For example, where sporting teams are keen to excel, team members and the coaching staff keep under constant review the game plan, basic strategies, player fitness and attitudes, and pre-match preparation routines. They have a 'theory' about what it takes to win that they are prepared to review and revise, sometimes quite drastically, if a fair measure of success is not enjoyed. Likewise, managers of business enterprises have 'theories' about how to improve profitability and services to clients which they implement with considerable enthusiasm. Where targets are not being met, they review their marketing strategies, client satisfaction levels, cost structures, product appeal, growth forecasts and the basic assumptions underlying earlier decisions about these matters, and make changes where necessary. These processes are seen as essential to ensuring that their businesses remain competitive and viable in a difficult trading environment. Thus a general principle, among those keen to lift performance and be recognized for quality, is to continually search for a new or improved *modus operandi* or theory of engagement.

In the world of teaching, similar processes occur. Where teachers have become highly effective, it is because they have regularly checked on the effects of what they do, looked for explanations for what's going well or not so well and reviewed and revised their practical theories and actions to meet new contextual requirements. Their self-critiques focus on a diversity of matters such as their plans, strategies, motives, goals, expectations, beliefs, values, hopes and their perceptions of students and themselves. To be effective, then, teachers have to make adjustments to their practical theories or 'what makes them tick' as teachers; they have to be their own mental technicians in a sense, checking on and refining the mental and moral structures that direct their professional work.

Reviewing, revising and perhaps even reformulating practical theories of teaching and the practices to which they give rise are far from simple. There are many complicating factors. For beginning teachers, the task is especially difficult because the changes they are sometimes called on to make may be prescribed by well-meaning superiors. Novices may be required to fit a stereotypical model of good teaching that they find unacceptable and to which they have no real commitment. Sometimes a change in practice is mandated without there being any attempt to develop the underlying theory. Even where the approach to improving effectiveness involves collaboration, negotiation, provision of professional support and a dual focus on the what and why of practice, there are still many problems. One of the main ones is that practical theories have usually not been fully articulated. In other words, teachers may not be aware of the 'theory' that underpins their practice. In fact, practical theories are somewhat analogous to icebergs. Each has large pieces residing below the surface, out of sight or out of mind. How then can teachers review and revise their practical theories if important parts of them are hidden or implicit? An obvious answer is for teachers to make the implicit explicit, that is, to bring to a conscious level that which has been out of awareness. That, too, is much more difficult than it sounds. Some of the various techniques which facilitate that process of articulation were outlined in the previous chapter. What renders the task somewhat easier is knowledge of the constituents of practical theories and how they are structured.

Focus of Chapter

In this chapter answers to the following questions will be sought:

- What do teachers talk about when they describe their practical theories?
- What constitutes their practical theories?
- What are the basic elements used by teachers in discussing their theories?
- What links, if any, are there among the elements?
- Do theories have a structure? If so, how are theories structured?

The answers to these questions will be illustrated mainly with details from the practical theories of various primary and secondary teachers who have collaborated with me in the documentation of their practical theories, but also from the research literature on practical theories. Unfortunately, none of these teachers was working in a distance education context. In fact, a thorough search of the relevant corpus of literature revealed not one report on the practical theories of distance teachers. For that reason, a teacher who

> works in the field of distance education at tertiary level was interviewed to
> provide one example of a practical theory of a distance teacher. It is important
> to note at this point that an assumption has been made that, though the
> substance of the practical theories of distance teachers as a group could
> well contain some unique features, most of the basic elements of practical
> theories as well as their structure would be common to all teachers.
> Throughout this chapter, readers will be encouraged to introspect, through
> a series of highly structured activities. These activities, called 'Invitations to
> reflect', are designed to assist readers to begin to document important aspects
> of their own practical theories of distance education.

Substance of Teachers' Practical Theories

Introduction

Answers to questions about the content and structure of teachers' practical theories of teaching can be found in the literature on teacher thinking. Hopefully, these answers will provide you with some clues about how best to represent your own practical theories, but it is important not to feel constrained by them. We should not feel obliged to try to make our own practical theories fit the moulds or constructs which others have found convenient. This is so because, in the first place, studies confirm the individualistic nature of theories and so cast some doubt on the usefulness of stereotypical models for representing practical theories. A second reason is that few of the moulds have been provided directly by teachers themselves. The various constructs which have been used to represent the practical theories of teachers have mostly emerged from careful analysis of what teachers say, but may not necessarily have been used or generated by them. In the main, they have come from researchers who have attempted to find ways of categorizing teacher talk about practical theories and who then have given their own labels to these categories. To be fair, most researchers confer extensively with their teacher-collaborators about the validity and naming of the categories but, in many instances, the labels employed come from codified knowledge in disciplines such as sociology and psychology. As a result, they may not represent with fidelity the ways teachers think about their work. For those and other reasons, the move to have teachers speak for themselves – the teacher voice movement (see Elbaz, 1991; Hargreaves, 1996) – has received considerable impetus. Clearly, for educational and professional reasons, as well as political and moral ones, it is important for the voices of teachers to be heard.

We need to be aware that assuming ownership of what others say in interviews – their intellectual capital – is knowledge colonization (Elbaz, 1991) which, as well as being presumptuous, carries with it certain risks and responsibilities. Moreover, we need to be sensitive to the ethics and risks involved in speaking for others. Among other potential problems, colonization of others' knowledge may result in misrepresentations of that knowledge. Another's account of what a teacher says may not carry the same emphases, nuances, feelings or qualities as those intended by the teacher. Those who have had their utterances misquoted or misrepresented by others know how offensive and damaging such instances can be. The conclusion to be drawn from this is that, in documenting your own practical theory, you should use only what has personal relevance and worth to you and avoid uncritical adoption of any of the moulds that have been used. With those cautions in mind, let us now review what studies of teachers' practical theories have revealed about their substance.

Concepts which are frequently used to communicate the substance of teachers' practical theories and which I have found in teacher discourse about why they teach the ways they do include:

- values and beliefs;
- goals;
- student states;
- cues;
- strategies;
- principles;
- teacher attributes;
- contextual factors;
- metaphors and images; and
- pedagogical content knowledge.

Values and beliefs

A large number of concepts have been used in attempts to encapsulate the essence and meaning of teachers' practical theories. Some of these have gradually lost currency while others have gained it. Among the most enduring of concepts are 'values' and 'beliefs'. These are important components in what Sockett (1987) calls the moral dimension of teaching or the moral framework within which our work as teachers is conducted. A similar point of view is expressed by Tom (1988) who describes teaching as a moral activity. Dill et al. (1990) point out, too, that one of the essential characteristics of a good teacher is 'fidelity to a set of values and an uncompromising effort to relate values professed to choices made' (p.151) and to actions planned. The values we hold, that is, the ideas in life we attach great value or importance to and try to live by, can have a pervasive and determining influence on the way we teach. For example, teachers who place a high value on students experiencing security, belongingness and respect will try to ensure that these values are reflected as often as they can be in the strategies and processes they use and the relationships they form with their students. Accordingly, one would expect that the classrooms of teachers who hold these values would be violence-free zones in terms of both verbal and physical abuse.

The power of values to shape teaching was also evidenced in the practical knowledge of Sue, a highly effective teacher of junior science and mathematics in a rural secondary school in Australia (Marland, 1994). Sue placed great value on what she called 'student welfare'. Her commitment to this value meant that she prized and respected her students. She saw herself as being 'there (in the school and classroom) for students'. Their well-being, which for Sue was closely bound up with notions of student independence, positive self-image and personal integrity, was the central focus of her lessons. Her concern for their welfare meant that she attached much importance to avoiding 'put-downs', shoring up their sense of personal worth and preserving positive student-teacher relationships, even at cost to herself. Venting anger and engaging in retaliatory behaviour, though they might have produced some psychological benefits for Sue, were not regarded by her as acceptable teacher behaviours in the classroom.

In teachers' value systems, not all values carry the same weight. Some tend to be more strongly subscribed to than others. In the past, considerable emphasis was placed on neatness, tidiness, conformity and compliance. Now, in many contemporary classrooms, these values are played down and a higher priority is placed on other values such as independence, initiative and creativity. For Sue, student welfare was a dominant value. So too was student capacity for independent thinking and action. She wanted them to think for themselves, to take responsibility for their own actions, to retain a healthy scepticism and not to accept things just because they were said by people in authority. Evidence of this capacity in students was valued more highly by Sue than ratings on science tests and coverage of the content in the science curriculum.

Sometimes, teachers find it difficult to decide on the pecking order among their values. Glenda, a grade 12 teacher of English, attached great importance to both coverage of the curriculum content and to class discussion (Marland and Osborne, 1990). Consequently, she often faced a dilemma because allowing prolonged but valuable discussion in a lesson threatened full content coverage. Deciding whether to terminate a lively discussion among students in the interest of covering all the content, or to allow it to continue, was an issue which she found difficult to resolve because she attached value to both. This dilemma arose because of uncertainty about which of the two values should be given priority. In the end, decisions about which alternative should be followed would probably be made in the light of the specific circumstances in which the dilemma arose, but at least the options were clear and the decision making about which option should be followed was informed by consciously-held values.

Dilemma management is a difficult process, and handling dilemmas is not an uncommon event in teachers' professional lives (Lampert, 1985). What makes dilemmas easier to manage, as well as practice more professional, is awareness of the relevant values. Teachers who are clear about the values they hold will not only be able to manage dilemmas more effectively but also be able to take decisions and actions more in line with those values. Being clear about the values one holds also provides a clear vantage point for reviewing one's practices and decisions to ensure congruence between values and practice.

Values are often associated or aligned with sets of beliefs. For example, the value many educators place on preparation of lessons and resources is usually justified by reference to a set of beliefs such as:

Careful preparation:

- allows for effective use of classroom time;
- provides teachers with a sense of confidence which is often transmitted in lessons;
- allows teachers to anticipate, and prepare for, what might happen in the lesson; and
- enhances the effectiveness of teaching and learning.

Similarly, many distance educators attach much worth to advance organizers because they believe that they provide students with a useful map of the content to be covered, allow for the integration of new and old material, and promote meaningful learning.

The beliefs and belief systems of teachers continue to be the focus of attention in professional development programmes, as well as in research on teachers' knowledge. This is because beliefs, or what teachers have faith or confidence in, play a key role in influencing the approaches adopted by teachers (Brickhouse, 1990; Bussis et al., 1976). Recognition of this role can be seen in a model of teacher thought and action proposed by Clark and Peterson (1986) and in Gage's (1978) earlier conceptualization of the nature of teachers' theories. Teachers who believe that students learn by doing are likely to incorporate practical activities into the learning opportunities they provide, wherever feasible. A distance teacher who believes that dialogue among learners about content promotes understanding and deeper insights into the material will very likely set up teleconferences, circulate e-mail addresses to facilitate exchange of ideas, encourage study groups and arrange meetings for groups of students. On the other hand, if teachers do not confidently believe that certain strategies will prove worthwhile or be effective, they are not likely to use them.

Although actions are usually grounded in beliefs, this is not always the case. Some teaching practices are based on tradition or routines for which the rationale has long been forgotten. Where this happens, there is the possibility that practices may lose their relevance or have their purpose distorted. At the same time, teachers may sometimes be required, through legislation or policy directives, to adopt practices which they do not believe in or which they oppose ideologically or professionally. In these instances, compliance may be less than wholehearted and actions only a flawed and incomplete expression of what was intended.

There are, of course, many other reasons for a lack of congruence between beliefs and actions. Sometimes it is not possible or desirable for beliefs to be translated into action, for reasons to do with lack of funds or resources, the absence of appropriate conditions or the impracticality of operationalizing the belief. Whatever the reason, it needs to be examined for validity or acceptability. What would be difficult to accept would be a lack of congruency between belief and action originating from oversight, neglect or lack of professionalism.

Sometimes, however, the beliefs underpinning practice can be flawed or erroneous. Novice distance teachers might believe, for example, that their students will proceed through the printed materials, segment by segment, in linear fashion. The materials they prepare, including study and assessment activities, may reflect this belief. However, research into the study habits of distance students reveals that this is not the case: students use a variety of starting points and follow very different routes through the material. Awareness of the varied patterns of student use may call into question the appropriateness of the access structure and other features built into the printed materials, as well as challenging the belief about linearity in student progress.

Another example of a questionable belief comes from a study of students' in-class thinking (Marland and Edwards, 1986). The teacher of a grade 11 biology class in this study used to respond to student questions by probes which were intended to assist the students to discover the answers to their own questions. The practice was based on a belief that probing was an effective tool to use in aiding understanding, a belief with some research backing (Dunkin and Biddle, 1974). Access to the in-class thinking of students showed a very different appreciation of probing among students. They disliked it intensely, seeing it, to use their words, as tantamount to 'being put in a mental torture chamber'. For these adolescent students, being probed by the teacher lay them open to having to admit not knowing something and hence to public humiliation or embarrassment. Understandably, the effect of probing on this class was to deter student-initiated questions and attempts to seek clarification of ideas. They were simply unprepared to ask questions because the inevitable result was that they would be probed. Clearly, beliefs and the actions based on them need to be subjected to careful scrutiny because even those with an apparently sound logical or empirical pedigree may not hold up under detailed examination as worthwhile in some contexts.

Beliefs, like values, are not easy to explicate, partly because they are so ingrained and deep-seated psychologically, but also because of their number and diversity. It would be difficult to catalogue all the beliefs which underpin our individual approaches to teaching. Even listing the broad fields within which beliefs might be categorized would be a daunting task. Perhaps a reasonable approach to the identification of beliefs would be to document the principal beliefs we hold in some of the key areas. Those areas might include planning; the nature of learners and learning processes; teaching strategies, including ones for motivating and challenging; management principles, including reward, punishment and discipline; relationships with students; assessment practices and the place of feedback; and ways of providing learners with access to content to be learned.

One last point about beliefs should be noted. They are very durable and resistant to change. It is not easy for teachers to shed or modify beliefs which have been part of their thinking for a long time. Thus, one of the major challenges we face in changing the way we teach is changing the values and beliefs which we have become so attached to and dependent on.

Invitation to Reflect

Set down the principal values within your practical theory of distance education, that is the ones that underpin your approach to distance education. Do you have any values that relate to:

- Support for learners?
- Features in distance materials?
- Types of learning?
- Relationships with students?
- Contacts among students?
- Learning outcomes?
- Assessment and feedback?
- Use and place of technology?

One of the critically important domains for values and beliefs is learning, because the type or types of learning you value and the beliefs you hold about how learning occurs will affect the strategies you employ, the expectations you set, the design of assessment tasks, feedback provided to students and, in distance education, the nature of study activities built into the learning materials. What kind(s) of learning do you value:

- Discovery learning?
- Learning of facts?
- Learning to apply knowledge?
- Rote learning?
- Learning how to learn?
- Self-initiated learning?

How do you believe learning occurs: by –

- Repetition?
- Relating new knowledge to old?
- Trying things out in practice?
- Discussion?

For each of the core values in your practical theory, set down the associated beliefs. For example, let us assume that you see great value in objectives. What is that valuing of objectives based on? You may believe that objectives:

- Provide students with a sense of direction.
- Offer you an important basis for the construction of assessment activities.
- Allow students to check on the outcomes of their study.

Please note: You will be provided with approaches to assessing your own practical theory in subsequent parts of this text.

Goals

When teachers explain why they teach the way they do, they inevitably make reference to their teaching goals or what they are trying to achieve for or with students. This, not unexpectedly, has been reported in a number of studies of teachers' practical knowledge, most recently by Cooper and McIntyre (1996) who referred to the statements of direction made by teachers in talk about teaching as 'aims'. Although teachers are probably aware of the broad aims of education as recorded in curriculum documents, those of the subjects they teach and the numerous objectives into which aims are translated, they tend not to cite these when discussing the basis for their approach to teaching (outlining their practical theories). Instead, they generally refer to a small number of key, broad, long-term goals which help to identify, and are consistent with, their own perspectives and missions as educators as well as those of the educational system in which they are serving.

These goals appear to be what teachers view as the dominant or superordinate goals. For example, Janesick (1977), in a seven-month ethnographic study of one American primary teacher, found that the teacher's approach was dominated by a commitment to creating and maintaining a cohesive and stable class. Recently, a similar goal was declared by the teaching principal of a multi-age class in a two-teacher school in rural Australia. The teacher, who was involved in a study of the practical knowledge base of highly effective teachers in multi-age classrooms (Marland et al., 1994), indicated that he was working towards establishing team spirit in his classroom and school. At the same time, within that cooperative environment, the teacher wanted students to develop as independent learners because he saw independence as essential to making the most of learning opportunities in multi-grade classes and later in secondary education. Reference to a few dominant goals was also apparent in a study involving secondary teachers (see of Batten et al., 1993, Chapter 4).

Evidence from research on the practical knowledge of teachers tends to suggest that goals are an important component of teacher formulations about how they teach. Furthermore, teacher discourse about what they are seeking to achieve in their teaching is dominated by reference to a small number of superordinate goals which they have singled out as being highly significant.

> **Invitation to Reflect**
>
> Write down what you consider to be the dominant goals in your approach to distance education. Be sure to identify those goals which are related to the specific professional context in which you work as a distance educator.
>
> Are any of the following goals compatible with your own approach to distance education:
>
> - To improve the practical skills of learners?
> - To teach learners to be sceptical and reflective?
> - To acquaint learners with knowledge and theory?
> - To develop capacities for group problem-solving, critical thinking or cooperative learning?
> - To enhance employment opportunities for learners?
> - To promote deep learning?

Student states

Brown and McIntyre (1988), in a study of the craft knowledge of some UK primary and secondary teachers whom their students had identified as good teachers, found that the teachers in their sample made reference to 'maintaining some kind of *normal desirable state of pupil activity*' when talking about and evaluating their teaching. The student states considered desirable varied from teacher to teacher. Attentiveness, involvement, motivation and volunteering responses to teacher questions were important to one teacher but, to another, important states included independence in learning, task-oriented behaviour and self-discipline.

Secondary teachers in an Australian project (Batten *et al.*, 1993), modelled on the Brown and McIntyre (1988) study, also referred to student states in their conceptualizations of teaching. A speech and drama teacher in this study, for example, listed imagination and generation of ideas, productivity and task-orientedness of groups, and willingness to compromise in the preparation of group products as student states that facilitated goal attainment in lessons and that contributed to successful learning and teaching.

Teachers in the Australian study, without any encouragement from the interviewer, also identified student states which could threaten attainment of goals and lesson success:

> For one teacher it was student apathy, disruptive behaviour, frequent changes in students' emotional states and over-dependence on the teacher.... For another it was student embarrassment, students resorting to deceptions to hide their lack of understanding and student boredom. (pp.37, 41)

It would seem, then, that teachers recognize that the cognitive and affective states of students are important influences on the directions lessons take and on opportunities for student learning. For this reason, they have developed tactics or techniques which facilitate the development of desirable states and others which inhibit the establishment of undesirable ones. Because student states can be both positive and negative influences on lesson events, the term used by Brown and McIntyre, 'normal desirable states', has been dropped in favour of one which covers both desirable and undesirable states.

Although the concept of 'student state' clearly has a place in practical theories of teachers involved in face-to-face teaching, its relevance to practical theories of distance teachers may not be quite so obvious at first glance. However, a persuasive argument can be made for regarding the notion as just as important in distance education. The distance teacher still has to try to induce those student states which are seen as integral to success in study or to prevent those which are inimical to student progress. For example, few would dispute that states of attentiveness, motivation and self-confidence in one's capacity to learn would be concomitants of successful distance learning. The challenge is to find how the distance teacher can create and maintain these states in students. On the other hand, it is well known that the relatively high attrition rate of students new to distance learning can be attributed to the sense of isolation they feel, the lack of stimulation from not being part of a student discussion group and the difficulty of obtaining regular feedback on problems as they arise. If these states of mind are allowed to develop, many able students may become disillusioned and consider forsaking their study. What steps can the distance teacher take to prevent these states of mind emerging in students?

Invitation to Reflect

Write down those student states of mind that you see as essential to success in distance learning. Would you want students to be:

- Critical?
- Sceptical?
- Inquiry-oriented?
- Introspective?
- Prepared to take initiatives?
- Imaginative?
- Flexible?

What student states do you see as harmful to their success in distance learning? Does it matter if distance learning materials cause students to feel:

- Overwhelmed?
- Confused?
- Intimidated by demands and terminology?
- Uncertain about how to obtain assistance?
- Reluctant to approach lecturers or peers?
- Frustrated?

If we are clear about the states of mind we want to induce in students and those we want to help students avoid, we should then be well placed to consider what we could do to promote desirable states and inhibit undesirable ones in students. Likewise, if we have made explicit our values, beliefs and goals, we have frames of reference within which we can begin considering the means we are going to employ to achieve our ends.

Cues

Research I have conducted on teachers' practical theories suggests that teachers gauge the affective and cognitive states students are in by making reference to verbal and non-verbal indicators or cues, also referred to by different teachers as signs, signals and messages. These cues, to which teachers assign their own particular meanings, are seen by teachers as important keys to teaching effectiveness. Indeed, many of the studies I have undertaken which have sought to document the practical theories of a range of highly effective teachers suggest that these teachers are particularly cue-conscious. They are always on the look-out for cues which provide feedback on how students are thinking and feeling and hence about the success of the lesson, or lack of it, and student learning. Teachers report that they use cues to gain insights into how students are thinking and feeling, insights which are then used to shape subsequent teaching behaviours and to make decisions, even quite radical ones, about the pace or direction of a lesson.

The cues which teachers look for can often be provided by a group or groups of students within the class. In the study of ten highly effective teachers of junior science and mathematics (Marland, 1994), one of the science teachers, for example, monitored students as they entered the classroom and then noted such things as where they sat, who they sat next to, whether they maintained eye contact with her, their body posture and level of participation in discussion. Some of the messages these cues conveyed to the teacher had to do with students' level of interest, enthusiasm, dislike of the topic, task orientation, degree of concentration, understanding or a desire to be left alone. The teacher then used these 'messages' or interpretations to tailor her responses to, or interactions with, individual students, a group, or the class as a whole. Her sensitivity to cues and student states was aimed at maintaining and improving teacher-student relationships, optimizing conditions for learning and nurturing the psychological well-being of students. This use of cues was similar to the 'mood assessment' strategy reported by a grade 12 teacher of English (Marland and Osborne, 1990) who began identifying and assessing student cues as soon as she entered the classroom and who would then adopt a strategy to begin the lesson that suited the mood of the class as she perceived it. Another of the teachers in the previous study, a teacher of mathematics, used a variety of cues, such as 'a funny inquiring look', a 'roundabout question from a student', level of involvement, interest, enthusiasm and a preparedness to do extra work, to identify 'teachable moments', peak times when students were ready and willing to learn. An absence of such cues during lessons prompted a review of his teaching strategies. 'If the indicators are not there... then perhaps I'm not choosing examples, telling enough stories that will switch them on (or) I'm not using a variety of teaching strategies and I need to widen the variety' (p.15).

Teachers have also indicated an interest in cues from individual class members as a means of determining the best way of handling that student. Interpretation of cues from an individual student often appears to be based on the knowledge that the teacher has accumulated on that student and is used to tailor the teacher's response to, or treatment of, the student. In the case study of one teacher of secondary English (Marland and Osborne, 1990), the teacher 'used her rich store of knowledge of students to interpret their individual behaviours and then often to plan reactions that were customised or tailor-made to suit particular individuals' (p.107).

Studies of teachers' practical theories have led me to conclude that, for classroom teachers – those who have regular face-to-face contact with their students – cues and their interpretation are very important features of their practical theories. Whether this is true to the same extent for distance teachers is perhaps open to question. By comparison with teachers in regular classrooms, the distance teacher has fewer opportunities to pick up student cues because contacts with students are more infrequent, less sustained and rarely, if ever, face-to-face. Moreover, for these reasons too, the distance teacher may have a less extensive inventory of knowledge about individual students. Consequently, this thinner database might make cue interpretation more problematic. Presumably, cues identified by distance teachers in contacts with their students would still provide useful indicators of student states which, in turn, would prove useful in interacting with distance learners in teleconferences, phone calls and written comments. The extent to which cues and cue interpretation are important components of the practical theories of distance teachers will probably be dependent on the quantity and quality of contacts between distance teacher and distance learner.

> ### Invitation to Reflect
>
> In the preceding activity, you were asked to identify those student states which facilitate successful learning and which you would try to induce in your distance students. Take each of those student states and identify the student cues that would indicate to you that students were in those states. For example, what cues would indicate to you that your students were:
>
> - Challenged by the distance materials you had developed?
> - Prepared to give open-ended consideration to a crucial topic or proposition?
> - Willing to reflect critically on their own workplace practices?
>
> Now take those student states that might inhibit student learning and that you are trying to prevent. What student cues would indicate to you that they might be in, or about to enter, those states? For example, what cues would indicate to you that your students were:
>
> - Feeling overwhelmed by the amount of work they have to complete?
> - Frustrated by some aspect of the distance course such as difficult terminology, apparent irrelevance of the study material or complex assessment tasks?
> - Confused by different advice from staff associated with the subject or course?
>
> A related question concerns opportunities students have for registering those cues.
>
> - In how many different ways and how frequently do you provide students with opportunities for indicating their affective and cognitive states?
> - Are they invited or encouraged to indicate how they are thinking and feeling?

Strategies

The means that are employed to help learners fulfil educational goals and needs represent what is generally acknowledged as a crucial element in practical theories of teaching. This element has been referred to by a variety of terms all of which, in this book, will be placed under the rubric of 'strategies'. These terms include models of teaching (Joyce and Weil, 1992), actions (Brown and McIntyre, 1988), performance (Cooper and McIntyre, 1996), and tactics (Batten *et al.*, 1993). These terms range from the macro or more inclusive ones such as 'model of teaching' and 'performance' to the micro or less inclusive ones like 'tactic'.

A model of teaching, as conceptualized by Joyce and Weil (1992), contains quite a number of components, including goal focus, phasing, social system and support system; performance has been defined by Cooper and McIntyre (1996) as including 'decisions made in proactive and/or interactive phases of lessons, their [teachers'] management and presentation skills, and the success and appropriateness of their teaching methods' (p.78). The term 'tactic', on the other hand, is usually taken as describing those small-scale, specific behaviours which teachers engage in from moment to moment.

The same diversity in terminology is found among practitioners. However, though teachers occasionally use the broader, more inclusive terms – Glenda, for example, spoke about her 'theory of talk', which encompassed goals, tactics and some basic propositions about teaching-learning links (Marland and Osborne, 1990) – much teacher talk about educational means tends to involve terms like strategies, methods and tactics. Some illustrations are provided below.

A grade 10 teacher of history in the study by Batten *et al.* (1993), referred to as teacher C, described clusters of tactics which served important purposes within the classroom. She had tactics for:

- countering student apathy;
- fostering student enthusiasm;
- handling variations in cooperativeness;
- encouraging students to be more responsible;
- coping with constantly changing emotional states of students;
- getting students to work independently; and
- handling disruptive students.

Valuable aids to learning and understanding, listed by both teachers and students in the study by Cooper and McIntyre (1996), were referred to as 'methods'. These included:

- explication by the teacher of lesson agendas;
- teacher recapitulation of previous lesson and establishing links between lessons;
- group work and working in pairs;
- role plays and drama; and
- teacher explanations accompanied by discussion and question-and-answer sessions.

A third example comes from Allan, a junior secondary teacher of science (Marland, 1994), who identified ten methods within his overall approach to teaching. These methods covered ways of teaching designed to promote concept development, promote development of student responsibility, encourage independent research skills, enable and foster a sense of belonging, input new content, check understanding, provide fun experiences in class, get students focused, motivate students, and facilitate success. Operationalizing each of these methods usually involved a number of key processes. Those for facilitating success, for example, were:

- basing a lesson on a sound structure;
- pitching material at the right level;
- reinforcing appropriate student behaviour;
- giving appropriate feedback, including knowledge of academic results; and
- developing a sense of trust in the teacher's competence.

There was yet another dimension or level to Allan's practical knowledge of strategies. Each of the processes had been further differentiated so that, to develop student trust for example, Allan believed he had to be well prepared; display competence by showing that 'he knew his stuff'; be able to predict where students would have trouble; allow students to ask questions with total impunity and without the fear of being put down; and declare to students that he could be trusted and then make sure he lived up to his claim.

As we have seen above, some teachers tend to describe their strategies in terms of the functions they serve. Allan, for example, had strategies for developing concepts or inputting new content or providing fun experiences. Broader categories have also been used to describe the functions of teaching strategies. A four-way classification of models of teaching based on goal orientation was proposed by Joyce and Weil (1992). Models were classified according to whether the goals they were serving were predominantly related to the acquisition of information and information-processing skills, social interaction, development of personal potential or management of student behaviour. Simple two-way classifications, such as progressive versus traditional or formal versus informal (Bennett, 1976), have also been used. Perhaps the most current of these is the open versus closed classification where open methods are broadly described as those which maximize student choice and closed methods as those which limit student choice. The relative merits of both types, and the values on which both are based, have been the substance of protracted and heated debate over the last two decades. Because the issue is still very much a contemporary one, and of considerable importance in an era when flexibility is of paramount concern in the delivery of courses, especially at the tertiary level, it will be revisited at a later point in this book.

Strategies in distance education

The material we have reviewed on teaching strategies has come mainly from the discursive and research literature on teaching, including research into the practical knowledge of teachers who have face-to-face contact with students. However, the issue of what strategies to use is no less important for distance teachers. The principal difference is that distance teachers have to embed their strategies in the learning materials they prepare and so have an indirect role to play in the implementation of those strategies, rather than a direct, hands-on one. The distance teacher cannot be physically there with the learner or group of learners in their 'classrooms' but can still exert an influence through the media they use. Hence, distance teachers can structure the design of their distance materials round a diverse set of strategies such as field studies, laboratory practicals, group work, individual research and role plays.

Learning from discussions among distance students or between them and distance teachers can be promoted via telephone or video links. In-class tutorials can be simulated in the package of learning materials through a printed version of a tutorial, referred to as a tutorial-in-print (Rowntree, 1992):

> Like a good human tutor, the package tells the learner what they are supposed to get out of the session, and then explains the subject clearly with examples that tie in to their experience... Like a tutor, it asks the learner frequent questions to check that they have understood the ideas being discussed and can comment on them or use them (p.134).

As we shall see later, it is possible to engage distance learners in group problem-solving, role-plays and cooperative learning as well as strategies requiring more independent work. In addition, many of the conventional strategies commonly used in face-to-face teaching, such as overviews, pre-tests, advance organizers and summaries can be adapted to suit the distance education context (Marland and Store, 1993). In fact, many of the strategies which teachers use in classrooms can find, after some metamorphosis, a useful place in distance education.

Invitation to Reflect

List the teaching strategies that you would want to use in the distance materials you prepare. Which of the following strategies would you consider appropriate in your distance programme:

- Brain-storming?
- Project work?
- Group investigation?
- Negotiating assessment activities?
- Motivating students?
- Use of verbal emphasis?
- Structuring?
- Study of interactive multimedia materials?
- Summarizing?
- Experimentation?

How would you plan to have students implement those strategies and to monitor them?

How do you intend generating your list of strategies? At some stage, it may be necessary to refer to your own goals, basic values and beliefs to ensure that strategies are consistent with those elements. Would it be helpful to identify some of the important pedagogical issues to be addressed in distance teaching? In this regard, are any of the issues raised in the following questions of importance to you?

- How do you orient distance learners to what your course or subject is about?
- How do you signify what is critically important in the content?
- How do you encourage student independence?
- How do you indicate what students have to do to complete the subject satisfactorily?
- How do you want students to interact with the content in order to achieve the outcomes? Through reading? Discussion? Field trials?
- How do you promote the kind of student learning considered appropriate in your subject?

There may be other more important questions you think you should be answering. What are they?

Principles

When teachers disclose their practical knowledge about strategies, they often make statements about the guidelines which they use to direct their behaviour. These guidelines, which have wide applicability and are usually consistent with values and beliefs, are referred to as 'principles'. Principles have been reported in a number of studies of teacher thinking (Clark and Peterson, 1986). Two of these studies reported that the principle of suppressing or 'keeping the lid on' emotions had been enunciated by several primary teachers. These teachers considered it generally unwise for them to give full, overt expression to the emotions they experienced during lessons because it could quite easily overly excite students and give rise to management problems. Other teachers invoked the principle of strategic leniency which involved them in sometimes overlooking student misdemeanours where they felt the student was in need of special consideration. Hence these teachers sometimes regarded bending the rules by being lenient with some students as the right thing to do strategically, because application of the rules could do more harm than non-application. Moreover, these teachers felt that their leniency would probably be endorsed by other students in the class.

One principle which used to be part of pedagogical folklore and was communicated readily to all novice teachers by their experienced colleagues was: 'Don't smile till Christmas'. The version used in the southern hemisphere, where the school year commences in January, is: 'Don't smile till Easter'. Whether this principle still holds, or should hold, an important place in the minds of practitioners is open to question. Some may consider that, in a period of greater informality and more openness in education, it no longer represents good practice.

What, then, are the principles that underpin the strategies you use in distance education? The next activity invites you to set down some of your basic principles.

> ### Invitation to Reflect
>
> Consider the following questions. Your answers may help you identify some of the principles on which your approach to distance teaching is based.
>
> - Where do you place objectives – at the start or end of your distance materials?
> - Do you state your own position on controversial issues in the materials you prepare or do you refrain from doing so?
> - Do you include model answers in your distance materials?
> - Do you provide students with copies of exemplary assignments? If so, when?
> - How frequently do you insert study activities/in-text questions/self-assessment questions in your distance materials?
> - How often do you contact students and seek feedback from them on their progress?
>
> What principles do you abide by in relation to:
>
> - Setting and marking assignments?
> - Providing students with access to your time?
> - The diversity of learning activities you build into your materials?
> - Setting work-load requirements for students?
>
> What other important aspects of distance teaching do you hold principles for? What are those principles?

Teacher attributes

In discussions of their practical theories, teachers report how their own personal attributes influence their choice and use of strategies and the effectiveness of that usage. The teacher who knows he or she has a good sense of humour, for example, and who believes that it can be used to improve teacher-student relations and student task-orientation, will seek to use that characteristic to advantage in the classroom. The same applies to teachers with a range of other attributes such as warmth and approachability, subject matter strengths, personal interests eg, in debating or abseiling, artistic ability, creativity and sporting prowess. Teachers are aware how they can use their attributes to good effect in the classroom. At the same time, the strategies teachers use can reflect an awareness of limitations or missing attributes. The teacher who knows that he or she does not have strong dramatic abilities may arrange learning opportunities in a way that draws on the acting talents of others.

It is important to recognize, in one's own attributes, areas of strength and limitation and to show recognition of these in the strategies we employ. It is also important to develop those attributes which we consider necessary for effective implementation of a strategy but which we lack or have little of.

Invitation to Reflect

Identify the attributes you have which could have an important bearing on your approach to distance education. Are you:

- Creative?
- Entrepreneurial?
- Practical?
- Easy to relate to?
- Charismatic?
- Innovative?

How is possession or absence of these attributes reflected in your distance teaching to enhance its potential to assist distance learning?

Which attributes do you have which you could make better use of in your distance teaching?

Contextual factors

For at least 20 years there has been recognition in research circles of the important part that contextual variables play in determining the nature and effectiveness of teaching and learning. This can be seen in the model for classroom research proposed by Dunkin and Biddle (1974), a model which directed attention to the importance of contextual factors in shaping teaching and learning and which exerted a pervasive influence on research into teaching from that time. This same recognition is clear in studies which report on teachers' conceptions of how teaching works (Batten *et al.*1993; Brown and McIntyre, 1988; Elbaz, 1983; Marland and Osborne, 1990). These studies indicate that teachers are keenly aware of how contextual factors affect the nature and success of their teaching and how their teaching has to be adjusted to suit the different environments in which they teach. In the Scottish study by Brown and McIntyre (1988) for example, teachers recounted how their teaching strategies were affected by the conditions impinging on themselves, students, content and what they taught. These conditions related to time, physical resources and conditions, the weather, the moods of students, the emotional and physical state of the teacher and content of the subject, course or unit of work. Other studies have extended the list of contextual factors affecting teaching and learning to include the school, the families of students, the community and the school system, to name but a few.

In the accounts of teachers' practical theories, there is substantial evidence that teachers acknowledge that the way they teach has to accommodate these contextual factors, some of which are capricious and unpredictable. In other words, the practical theories that teachers hold reflect the view that pedagogy must be adjusted in response to, or in anticipation of, the impacts of a wide range of contextual factors. An example of this can be seen in the flexible approach to starting lessons reported by Glenda, a grade 12 English teacher (Marland and Osborne, 1990). On entering the classroom, this teacher looked for cues which would allow her to make some judgement about the prevailing mood of the classroom. After assessing the mood of the class, the teacher would then adopt an approach to starting the lesson which she considered the most appropriate for that particular mood – formal, businesslike and highly structured if she considered the class 'flighty'; more interactive, relaxed and less structured if she assessed them as ready for discussion, and so on.

This example, as well as showing how contextual factors can influence a teacher's choice of strategy, illustrates the importance of the teacher's knowledge of her students (students are often represented as the most significant aspect of the context). Indeed, without an in-depth knowledge of individual students, the cues they emit in the classroom and the meanings of those cues, Glenda's assessment of student moods could well have been called into question. This would also have cast some doubt on the appropriateness of the particular strategies chosen. In fact, a rich base of knowledge about students is probably essential to accurate interpretation of the cues that students provide and to setting up optimum conditions for learning. Some research is beginning to suggest that teaching effectiveness is linked to a detailed, personal or close-to-clinical knowledge of individual students (Mayer *et al.*, 1994). Following a study of expert primary teachers of composite (two-grade) classes in New South Wales, Phillips *et al.* (1993) concluded that 'one of the major reasons these teachers were outstanding was because they knew and understood each child so well and they used this knowledge to manage, correct and stimulate children's learning' (p.15).

Now, of course, the distance education environment is very different from that encountered in classrooms in schools and universities populated by teachers and day or on-campus students. Distance students and their teachers rarely, if ever, meet; access to resources may be limited or difficult to arrange; and communications between the two groups may be punctuated by delays. Clearly, there are many contextual factors which will affect the provision of distance teaching – means of communication, student access to computers and other resources, institutional policies and practices and time – to name but a few. The distance educator needs to be aware of these and to develop strategies to accommodate them. Educational provisions must serve students in the best way possible, whether they are distance learners or physically present in classrooms.

> ### Invitation to Reflect
>
> From your point of view as a distance teacher, what are some of the main kinds of contextual factors that impinge on your distance teaching? Does you list include:
>
> - Time (time both you and the students can make available for the course or for study)?
> - Resources?
> - Means of communication?
> - Students?
>
> What might be some of the contextual factors that are of concern to students? Might they include:
>
> - Distance (eg, from the post office, the tutor, computer facilities, other students)?
> - Access to the distance teacher?
> - Are there any that you have overlooked?
>
> What do you need to know about the students who enrol, or are likely to enrol in your distance teaching courses in order to provide them with the best distance teaching materials you can design?
>
> Which of the following categories of knowledge of students would you consider important:
>
> - Prerequisite skills?
> - Employment?
> - Experience in distance study?
> - Residential location?
> - Family situation?
>
> How can these contextual factors be accommodated within your practical theory?

Metaphors and images

The above set of concepts which have been used to encapsulate major components of teachers' practical theories falls well short of a complete set. In describing and explaining what they do, teachers also make use of other constructs such as metaphors, images, rules, knots, routines and dilemmas. Only the first two will be discussed here.

Munby and Russell (1989) point out that teacher discourse about their work is full of metaphorical language and claim that this is so because the 'human conceptual system is defined and structured metaphorically... [and] human thought processes are largely metaphorical' (p.2). Hence, our internal representations of people, events and work, and our dialogue about these, are often expressed metaphorically. As Tiberius (1986) and others point out, an extensive range of metaphors, including teacher as cook, ship's captain, coach, travel agent and actor, has been used by teachers to represent their understanding of teaching and learning and the relationships between the two. The horticultural metaphor is used by some teachers to describe their role in promoting student growth (learning and development). Some teachers still see themselves as 'jug fillers', with learning viewed as a transmission process involving the relatively passive absorption by the learner of pieces of knowledge prepared and presented by the teacher. Sadly, what happens in classrooms is sometimes depicted by teachers in terms of the battle metaphor through words and phrases which denote the classroom as 'the trenches' and the learners as 'the other side' or 'the enemy'.

Because teachers tend to live by their metaphors (Tobin, 1990), the metaphorical language they use in talking about their teaching provides sharp insights into their practical theories. The metaphor adopted by a teacher can, in just a few words, define important aspects of teaching such as goals, strategies, conceptualizations of learning, values and beliefs, teacher-student relationships, and the role of the teacher, as well as showing the links among those aspects. The teacher who described herself as a social worker (Mayer *et al.*, 1994) because she regarded problems faced by students in their home as major impediments to learning and personal development, gave important insights into what were important aspects of her approach to teaching. Her practical theory included references to goals (eg, providing compensatory educational experiences for those with family and personal problems), key information she needed about students, techniques for gathering that information and important dimensions of her role (eg, observing students, gathering information on them, keeping close contact with parents), and learning activities for compensating those with social and personal problems (eg, team building, individual projects, high levels of teacher monitoring and supervision, and peer tutoring).

A second example is that of the science teacher who adopted a travel agent metaphor to give expression to her desire to move away from a teacher-centred approach towards one which placed greater emphasis on constructivist learning (Ritchie and Russell, 1991). The adoption of this metaphor allowed the teacher to define more clearly the implications of a constructivist approach for the roles of both teacher and students, techniques for motivating students to take learning trips, design of personally rewarding learning trips for students, management of resources and assessment and review of outcomes.

Sometimes, there is little awareness of the metaphors that guide our behaviours and shape our institutional structures. We may not even be aware of the negative consequences of the metaphors we live by. For centuries, the resources of our world have been exploited as though they were infinite. Now, the need to conserve, to recycle and to preserve has become more of an imperative as the metaphor of the world as a space capsule with finite resources gains ascendancy in global thinking. Over a quarter of a century ago, Toffler (1970) called into question the appropriateness of the factory metaphor as the basis for schooling. He drew some compelling parallels between schools and factories in terms of raw materials (learners) moving along conveyor belts (grades), components (knowledge and skills) being added piece by piece, whistles (bells) marking the start and end of production (teaching and learning) each day, shop-floor stewards (prefects and monitors) being responsible for workers (students) and basic processes, and quality control devices (examinations) being used to check on products (exiting students). Toffler described the plan to base schools on the factory model as a stroke of industrial genius because, from the point of view of factory owners, educating students in simulated factories provided an effective way of conditioning students to a working life in factories. Critics of the factory model for schooling pointed to the stress on uniformity and conformity, the lack of attention to individual needs and the depersonalizing effects of educational processes that were too mechanistic.

What then is an appropriate metaphor for education and for distance education? That is a question which all educators need to consider. It would be useful to examine our own teaching to identify the underlying metaphors, if we are not already familiar with them, and then to review their appropriateness. For example, if we find that practice is guided by the 'teacher as ship's captain' metaphor, is that appropriate? Adoption of this metaphor might mean exposing all passengers (students) to the delights (learning activities) of a fixed set of island destinations (subject topics). An alternative would be to adopt the 'teacher as travel agent' metaphor. This would at least allow teachers to help student voyagers design educational tours related to their own needs and interests.

In the 1990s, 'education as a business' appears to be a dominant metaphor. Though many educators may be discomforted by it, among politicians and governments it appears to have a good deal of appeal. Is this an appropriate metaphor for education? Should distance education enterprises be expected to grapple with what are essentially business-type issues such as efficiency, market share, economies of scale, profit margins, consumer demand and service quality? Does a focus on such concerns affect the integrity and quality of educational materials and processes? Is it appropriate for students to be regarded as consumers of educational products or clients of educational services? To what extent should client needs determine the shape and content of educational products? Should that which clients find unpalatable be omitted? If this is done, will the educational product be useful and serviceable? There are, of course, many other issues which could be raised in relation to the education as business metaphor. They will not be explored here. The point of raising them was to illustrate how the metaphors we live by as teachers need to be subjected to careful scrutiny to ensure that they are valid and educationally sound.

Descriptions and explanations of teaching are also given by teachers in terms of the images they hold (Calderhead and Robson, 1991; Clandinin, 1986; Johnson, 1990). An image can be as simple as a mental snapshot in memory of a particular incident which, because of its vividness and potency, has a lingering and significant influence on how the teacher operates. Clandinin's view of images is more complex. She sees images as mental coalescences of experiences which have aesthetic, moral and emotional dimensions. Images become important componentry within a teacher's *zeitgeist* and *modus operandi*. The significance of such a construct can be seen in the image of the 'classroom as home' held by Stephanie, one of the teachers in Clandinin's study. This image had a pervasive impact on her teaching. Stephanie's personal experience of home life as stimulating, secure and happy and her less than favourable reactions to the formality of educational programmes she experienced caused her to form a view that the classroom environment for lower primary children should be as much like a home as possible. This image from her past experiences carried over into the class she conducted, through the activities she arranged, the teacher–student relationships she facilitated and the classroom ethos she sought to develop.

There may be images formed from your own personal and professional experiences which could or do exert a significant influence on your own approach to teaching. It is as well to be aware of such images and to assess their place in your practical theory and contribution to your teaching and its effectiveness. The contribution may be positive as in the case of Stephanie above, or negative as in the case of the science teacher (Batten, *et al.*, 1993) whose vivid images, from her own life as a student, involved teachers who were accusatory, humiliating and insensitive. She vowed never to display the same behaviours but to give to students what she 'as a student, didn't get in the classroom situation' (p.42). On the other hand, the impact of images could, just as easily, be counterproductive. For example, you may have images of events in your own schooling which you have elected to recreate whenever conditions allow. You do this because the images carry with them feelings of pleasure, reward and pride and a sense of goodness or moral worth. However, when those events are repeated in contacts between you and your students, the impact on your students may have been much less favourable. However, you persist because the enduring images you have hold sway in your teaching.

Structure of Teachers' Practical Theories

So far in this chapter, many of the components or elements of teachers' practical theories have been identified and discussed. A theory, however, is not just a bundle of unrelated elements. Usually, in a theory, the elements are linked together through a system of relationships. Snow (1973), for example, defines a theory as consisting of 'a) a set of units... and b) a system of relationships among the units' (p.78). The elements of theories, therefore, are not isolated, independent and free-floating. They cohere and are linked together by different types of relationships. It is this set of relationships among elements that gives a theory its structure.

Teachers' practical theories are no exception. They, too, have structure, with elements being linked by such relationships as the 'if... then' relationship or the 'cause-effect' relationship. Teacher action is guided by knowledge of these inter-element relationships which may take the form of: 'If A (contextual variable) is present, then I do B (strategy)'; or 'C (student state) gives rise to D (goal)'. Of course, these linkages are rarely stated without some proviso or qualification. It is this knowledge of relationships which allows or encourages teachers to predict with some accuracy what will or will not work under certain conditions, what the best course of action is, when to act or defer action, what is likely to eventuate later if certain conditions are present now, what to do to achieve specific goals and so on. Knowledge of the links between elements provides a basis for teachers to develop plans, make judgements, take decisions, act on hunches, interpret incidents and to reflect on other events in their professional lives.

Few researchers have addressed the issue of the structure of teachers' practical theories. Those that have (Batten *et al.*, 1993; Brown and McIntyre, 1988; Cooper and McIntyre, 1996; Marland and Osborne, 1990) indicate that teachers recognize many relationships among elements in their practical theories. These include relationships between:

- contextual factors and strategies;
- strategies and student states;
- student states and goals;
- strategies and goals; and
- teacher attributes and strategies.

There is also, in teachers' talk about teaching, a clear indication of their acknowledgement of the strong influence of their values and beliefs on the strategies, goals, student states and other elements which they have identified within their practical theories. It is as if values and beliefs provide a moral framework within which the other elements of practical theories are set. Thus it would not be appropriate to represent values and beliefs as being separate from the other elements because values and beliefs in fact permeate the other elements. This feature in teacher talk about their practical theories ought to be preserved according to Sockett (1987). To ignore it would be to deny the importance of the moral dimension in teachers' accounts of why they teach as they do and to reduce teacher talk about practical theories to a merely paratechnical language.

A general model of the structure of teachers' practical theories is provided in Figure 2.1. This model shows most of the elements of practical theories common across teachers and at least some of the relationships among those elements. It also seeks to represent the way in which a teacher's values and beliefs permeate the other elements and provides a framework within which the other elements are set. It does not include reference to metaphors and images, not because they are regarded as trite, but because both these constructs tend to offer alternative or different ways of representing significant chunks of practical theories. They overlap and synthesize other elements of a practical theory and thus provide a more macro-view of those aspects. In other words, both image and metaphor describe portions of a practical theory which may cover a number of elements and their relationships. The 'teaching as entertaining' metaphor, for example, provides a perspective on teaching which could integrate material from such elements as 'goals', 'strategies' (including the roles of teacher and students), 'teacher attributes' and 'beliefs'.

Teachers' practical theories: substance and structure 41

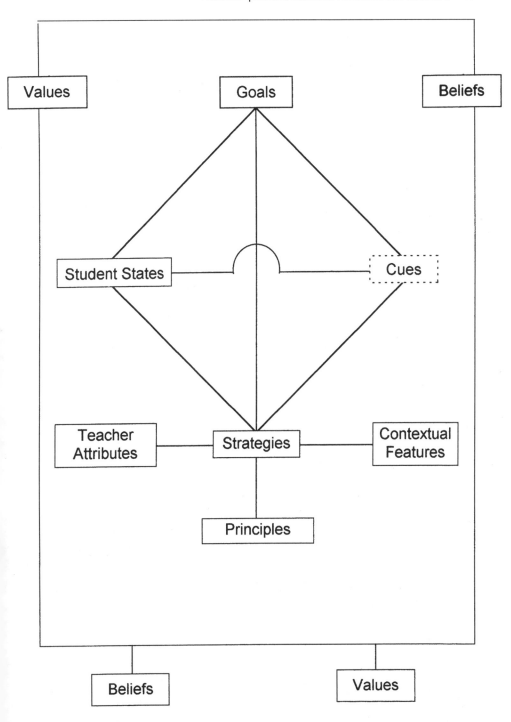

Figure 2.1 *Model of teachers' practical theories – components and structure*

Other Ways of Categorizing Teachers' Knowledge

It is important to note at this point that the practical knowledge which comprises teachers' practical theories, and which has been categorized above in terms of the elements of practical theories, has also been categorized in other ways. Elbaz (1983) proposed that the practical knowledge of teachers could be categorized into five domains: knowledge of curriculum; knowledge of instruction; knowledge of self; knowledge of subject matter; and knowledge of milieu. A similar set of domains was proposed by Grossman (1995) for teacher knowledge which subsumes, but is more extensive than, practical knowledge. Her typology of teacher knowledge included six knowledge domains: content; learners and learning; general pedagogy; curriculum; content; and self.

As Grossman points out, although the domains are represented as discrete, this separateness actually dissolves in practice, with teachers integrating knowledge from various domains when talking about and implementing their theories. As is evident from the terms used, these two systems for categorizing knowledge have much in common with each other. Also, both ways of categorizing teachers' knowledge have some loose parallels with elements of practical theories. For example, knowledge of self in the Elbaz and Grossman categorizations could be seen as subsuming, or perhaps even as roughly equivalent to, knowledge of one's own beliefs, values and attributes.

Pedagogical content knowledge

Shulman (1986) offered a similar list of knowledge domains but included one other, pedagogical content knowledge (PCK), which has been the focus of considerable research over recent years. This concept is a valuable one because it draws attention to a unique form of teacher knowledge and offers yet another way of integrating knowledge from different sources which has strong pedagogical relevance. PCK has been described as the content knowledge of subject matter 'teachers' rather than subject matter 'knowers' (Berliner, 1986). It is described by Shulman as a special blend of content knowledge and pedagogical knowledge, possessed only by teachers, which renders content into a communicable form for the benefits of learners; it enables teachers to 'elucidate subject matter in new ways, reorganise and partition it, clothe it in activities and emotions, in metaphor and exercises, and in examples and demonstrations, so that it can be grasped by students' (1987, p.13). By and large, PCK is the product of practice and so can be seen, partly at least, as practical knowledge.

Attempts have been made to document the pedagogical content knowledge of teachers and to identify the components of PCK. This has occurred in respect of a number of specific topics, including addition of fractions (Marks, 1990), social studies (Gudmonsdottir and Shulman, 1987) and novels (Grossman, 1988). Grossman's (1990) view of PCK as comprising four components – knowledge of curriculum, students, instructional strategies and the learning context – is still well-regarded (Fernandez-Balboa and Stiehl, 1995). However, it is important to remember that it is the integration, or the blending, of these knowledge components which provides the teacher with such a potent resource. The teacher with PCK not only has ways of transforming content into a learnable form through the use of metaphors, examples, analogies and other pedagogic devices but also has access to a knowledge of student interactions with that content which has the potential to further sharpen the appropriateness of the pedagogic approach and enhance the quality of the learning experience for students. This knowledge of student- content interactions covers such areas as what students find hard or easy, common errors made by students, ways students think about the content and the problems they encounter (Marks, 1990). The following anecdote illustrates the essence of PCK and the powerful contribution it can make to teaching effectiveness.

An example of PCK

The person in this anecdote was a teacher of history in a junior secondary class of girls and the material to be covered was related to World War I (WWI), with a special focus on its causes and consequences. The teacher was aware from past experience that the topic lacked appeal to female students in this age group. She was also aware of the less-than-enthusiastic student reactions to conventional approaches to teaching this unit of work such as using a direct instructional approach. Just before the series of lessons on WWI began, the teacher asked her female students to bring along a picture from a popular magazine of a 'spunky male'. For half the class, these male characters became fictitious 'boyfriends', 'brothers' or 'husbands' who had enlisted in the Australian Imperial Forces (AIF) and were on their way to Europe and the WWI battle zones. The other half of the class became the enlistees. Students were then asked to form pairs consisting of an enlistee and the enlistee's girlfriend, sister or wife. The teacher had the members of each pair correspond with each other, either about life in Australia or about experiences en route to Europe, on leave and in battle. In order to construct letters which accurately reflected the times, both groups, the AIF enlistees and their family members back home in Australia, had to engage in appropriate research. These letters, read out in class, were the focus of considerable discussion, allowing exchange of information about WWI, issues of that period to be debated and explored, and writing skills to be honed.

At appropriate times, the teacher would introduce to the class factual accounts of significant events in the prosecution of the war and the tragic circumstances for the army platoon in which the 'soldiers' were serving. Specific enlistees were nominated by the teacher as killed, missing-in-action, or injured, news which resulted in much genuine grief among members of the class who had begun to form strong bonds with their 'partners'. Thus, the objectives of the unit were met and in a way which impacted greatly on the class.

The knowledge displayed by the teacher in the anecdote appears to satisfy at least some of the requirements that Grossman has for PCK. It represented a blend of content knowledge and pedagogy – and a rather unusual blend at that – which had been tailored to meet some of the contextual difficulties and student reactions the teacher knew she would encounter in teaching this topic. From the point of view of the teacher, students and observer, the application of this piece of PCK had met with considerable success.

The relevance of this concept of pedagogical content knowledge to all teachers, including distance teachers, should be clear. In every subject, there will be many topics which can be taught and learnt more effectively if the wisdom of practice, in the form of PCK, is drawn on. Every opportunity should be taken, therefore, to seek out, develop and incorporate into distance learning materials this blend of content knowledge, knowledge of content-specific pedagogy and knowledge of typical student-content interactions.

The Practical Theory of a Distance Teacher – An Example

Introduction

Throughout this chapter, reference has been made to numerous studies of the practical theories of teachers. It was also noted, however, that a search of this literature failed to unearth one report of the practical theory of a distance teacher. Because it was felt that readers may derive some benefit from the presentation of a distance teacher's practical theory, a very brief exercise was undertaken to obtain such an account. The exercise involved seeking the assistance of a colleague who, in two half-hour conversations, provided some insights into the nature of his practical theory of distance teaching. Normally, studies which seek to document the practical theories of teachers would take very much longer and would supplement interviews with data obtained using other methods (see, for example, Marland and Osborne, 1990). However, severe time constraints allowed only a very brief time for data collection. As a result, the account of the practical theory of this distance teacher is limited to a description of the content or substance of the theory only. No attempt was made to have the distance teacher reveal the structure of his theory, though some of the links among elements will become apparent.

The colleague who assisted in this exercise, Dr David Ross, is an Associate Professor and Associate Director [Academic] within the Distance Education Centre of the University of Southern Queensland. As well as providing other university teachers with advice and assistance in the design and development of distance materials, he was also involved in distance teaching. The subject which was the focus of David's practical theory report was in the area of multimedia design and development and was offered to postgraduate students in the field of professional communication. The subject sought to provide students with interdisciplinary knowledge and skills in multimedia design, development and implementation and to make them aware of the social, political and economic contexts which had spawned the emergent media/communication industry.

Outline of David's practical theory
Values and beliefs
The approach adopted by David to the teaching of this subject reflected his commitment to three core values: activity-based learning, collaborative team work and a high level of student-student and student-lecturer interactivity. Though David acknowledged that the content of this subject does lend itself to a 'hands-on' approach, he insisted that even if he were asked to teach history, he would not lecture on history to the students. 'I would have interactive role-playing sessions; I would have more of an activity-based approach [so that students would get to] feel what history is all about'. His valuing of an activity-based approach stems partly from beliefs that such an approach assists with motivation of students, gives rise to better learning outcomes and makes it easier for them to meet objectives. Furthermore, David says, lecturers cannot 'deliver learning in the same way as postmen deliver letters' and so students have to 'find out for themselves'. Finding out for themselves, which probably has much in common with a constructivist approach to learning, involves, in David's view, seeking out information and taking initiatives independently, but also sharing with, and learning from, each other in teams. Not surprisingly, then, David values and promotes interaction among distance students and teachers. He believes that this simulates the dialogue between students and teachers in face-to-face classrooms and is a prerequisite for learning.

Other beliefs in key areas include the following:

Assessment
– Assessment is a way of learning.
– Assessment of students should be competency based, allowing students to repeat assignments five or six times if necessary.

Learning activities
– Activities which are too open-ended cause confusion among students.
– A print-based approach in this subject would produce more of a conceptual understanding rather than practical skills.
– Research indicates that activity-based learning has a high measure of success.
– Greater reliance should be placed on the Internet as a resource, marketing and sales tool and as a means of communication.

Industry expectations
– Students must show initiative because the industry in which they will eventually seek employment will require it of them.
– Students should be able to operate and manage multimedia projects.

Goals
Many of the superordinate goals David works towards reflect the values outlined above. He wants students to be good team members, able to establish an environment that will encourage participation by all. At the same time, he wants students to be able and willing to take initiatives, to be independent and

autonomous thinkers and to solve problems collaboratively. In addition to these goals, there are those which relate to the specific content of the subject, such as learning to use and apply principles of multimedia design and development, forming an appreciation of the power of multimedia as a way of promoting and marketing ideas, and developing an awareness of the requirements for establishing and operating policies for multimedia developments in industry.

Strategies and student states

David considered that a strategy that would enable his goals for the subject to be fulfilled would be to offer this subject via the Internet. This was a crucial strategic decision which appears consistent with at least some of his beliefs and values. It meant, however, that admission to the subject would be granted only to those distance students with access to computers of a certain kind. Students would also be required to have their own service providers but would receive, through the subject, the navigational tools they needed to 'surf the net'. One basic reason for the decision to use the Internet was that it would enable students to communicate electronically with each other and the lecturer, prepare 'home pages' to accommodate completed study and assessment tasks to which the lecturer would have access (without students having to post in their assignments), and draw on resources available through the Internet. Thus, the only print material to be issued would be that mailed out at the start of the subject to provide an overview and to help students get established on the Internet.

The second basic strategy which was seen as consistent with goals and would therefore be used in this subject was role-playing. All students who would be successfully enrolled in the subject would then be required to apply for positions as employees of a simulated company, Multimedia Advocacy Enterprises, of which David was the Chief Executive Officer (CEO). The student-employees would be answerable, individually and collectively, to him for the timely completion of activities, including design and development of multimedia products and the preparation of company documents such as mission statements, a set of company objectives, an organizational chart for the company and a statement of personnel requirements. The activities they were to complete would pose questions that required student-employees as a team to make decisions about what they were going to do. To satisfy these requirements of the company, the student-employees would have to interact extensively with each other and the CEO and engage in group decision making and problem solving.

In line with his beliefs, David planned to provide a minimum of content, opting instead to identify sources, Uniform Resource Locators (URLs), where students could obtain information or guidance (URLs can be viewed as the 'addresses' of documents and files on the Internet). Students would also be informed that they were expected to go beyond the resource locations provided, especially if, as company employees should be, they were committed to quality. In summary, then, the basic strategies David considered appropriate included use of technology; activity-based projects; and role-playing which would involve extensive interaction, decision making and problem solving.

As well as contributing to the attainment of goals, strategies were also seen as helping to inculcate certain student states. David wanted students to feel comfortable about team decision making and taking initiatives, to become committed to collaboration, to be attentive and sensitive to others yet prepared to be critical of the ideas of others, and to be inquiry-oriented. He wanted students to be willing to make contact with other students so that they could avoid a sense of being isolated and alone. Finally, he wanted students to think at a corporate level and to regard him as a CEO rather than as their lecturer and assessor. 'I hope that part of their thinking will be at a corporate level – at the upper management level. I want students to consider me as the leader of this company and not just the one who gives them grades at the end'. In fact, David envisaged his role as encompassing three main dimensions: as 'facilitator' of learning, as 'controller' of deadlines, quality processes and productivity, and as a 'standard setter'.

Principles

As the CEO, David planned to observe certain principles. He would frequently check on student progress by calling 'meetings'. He would give feedback to individuals and to teams but would seek to work collaboratively on problems rather than to be directive or dictatorial. 'Nothing is to be dictated to them [student-employees] as an authoritarian CEO'. However, he would be prepared to 'set tasks to put right problems arising from a lack of student involvement' because he viewed a lax student as a threat to team progress and success.

Another broad principle he would apply in the subject would be to simulate conditions experienced by employees within a company, as he was intent on preparing students for employment. Thus students would be rated on their productivity, in terms of both quality and quantity, and adherence to deadlines because those are important performance criteria in companies. Assessment tasks would also be designed with possible future employment contexts in mind. For example, the final assignment would require students to prepare, on their home pages, a multimedia commercial advertising a product idea that they have for the 'company'. Each student would also be required to make a presentation on a product idea during a computer conference to be arranged by the CEO. Another set of principles enunciated by David related to the design of activities. Two of these principles were:

- Ensure that distance materials incorporate a variety of learning activities.
- Design and sequence learning activities so that there is a gradual increase in levels of activity, interactivity, communication and complexity.

Teacher attributes

Teacher attributes that David saw as contributing to the success of strategies were interpersonal skills, confidence, flexibility and experience with the design and conduct of multimedia projects. Possession of these attributes would allow the CEO to relieve or smooth away the tensions or difficulties that inevitably arise in teams and to engender in students a sense of confidence in his leadership and advice and in the worthwhileness of their own projects and work products.

Contextual factors

All references made by David to contextual factors impinging on the way he planned to teach the subject related to students. He indicated that there were two main kinds of knowledge of potential clients that had been influential in determining the learning environment he sought to create and the strategies he intended to employ. These were knowledge of their academic backgrounds (particularly their entry level skills in video editing, audio digitizing and web-based publishing) and knowledge of some general characteristics of distance learners, specifically age, maturity and employment status.

Invitation to Reflect

The above outline of a practical theory of distance teaching, though somewhat attenuated because of restrictions on time for data collection, offers many insights into the rationale for the kinds of learning opportunities students would experience in this subject. Here are some matters to reflect on:

- How would your practical theory for this or a similar subject vary from this practical theory?
- Were the goals of this practical theory valid ones? Would you adopt different goals? If so, what justification would you give?
- Which of the basic values and beliefs do you share? Where do you differ? How would you defend those you espouse?
- Does this theory possess internal consistency? Are the prescribed means the most appropriate for achieving given ends? Do strategies reflect basic values? Are student states consistent with goals?
- Do you agree with the justifications given for requiring students to:
  - Use the Internet?
  - Engage in a role-play?
  - Interact with each other?
  - Work collaboratively?
  - Take initiatives?
  - Engage in group problem solving and decision making?
  - Meet strict work deadlines?
- If not, what changes would you make? What justifications would you give for these changes?
- Do you agree with the justifications given by the distance teacher for:
  - Maintaining regular contact with students?
  - Offering little by way of lecturer-written material to be studied?
  - Framing particular assessment requirements?
  - Adopting the role of a setter of standards?
- If not, what changes would you make? What justifications would you give for these changes?

Summary

The rationale for this chapter derives from a view widely held in contemporary education circles that improvements to the practice of distance teaching can be made only if the practical theories which underpin and shape each distance teacher's practice are subjected to careful scrutiny by the holder.

Such a proposition requires, as a first step, that distance teachers become fully conversant with their own practical theories of distance teaching. For that reason, this chapter has sought to describe and illustrate in detail many of the elements or components commonly found in teachers' practical theories of teaching. A generic model of teachers' practical theories was also presented to indicate some of the interrelationships that exist among the elements of these theories. Finally, the substance of one person's practical theory of distance teaching, held in respect of a postgraduate subject in professional communication, was outlined.

Throughout the chapter, readers were given numerous opportunities to reflect on the practical theories that shape their own approaches to distance teaching and to outline some of the principal features therein.

Chapter 3

Practical theories of teaching: review and revision

Review One of the basic premises on which this book is based is that teachers can make significant and durable improvements to the quality of their teaching if they are prepared to review and revise their practical theories of teaching. This requires that they regard their current practice as problematic, that they attend to the problems and paradoxes they identify within their professional practice and subject what they do and why they do it to critical scrutiny. Finally, it requires that they make changes to their practical theories and to the professional practice to which the theory gives expression.

The image of the teacher as a dynamic, quality-conscious, self-appraising professional, constantly striving for enhancement of teaching and learning, alluded to in the initial paragraph, is caught in Schön's (1983) notion of the 'reflective practitioner'.

Focus of Chapter

This chapter examines what it means for teachers to be reflective practitioners and what the review and revision of their practical theories of teaching entail. In particular, concepts of reflection-in-action, reflection-on-action, critical thinking and ways of promoting reflection, including action research, metaphors and journal writing will be explored. Although the treatment of these concepts will be necessarily brief, the expectation is that, by the end of this chapter, readers will have a keen insight into what the review and revision of their practical theories involve and will be equipped to subject their own practical theories of distance education to the processes of review and revision.

Introduction

Rethinking practical theories – a challenge

At this point, readers who have worked through the activities in Chapter 2 should now be reasonably clear about the substance and structure of their practical theories of distance education. The next challenge to consider is how to go about reviewing and revising practical theories so that the design of distance teaching materials and the provision of distance learning experiences can be enhanced.

Basis for a response to the challenge

A very useful response to this challenge comes from the work of Donald Schön (1983; 1987) who was interested in the kinds of knowing in which competent practitioners engage. Schön drew attention to a crisis of confidence in the professions in the early 1980s that seemed to be 'rooted in a growing skepticism about professional effectiveness in the larger sense, a skeptical reassessment of the professions' actual contribution to society's well-being through the delivery of competent services based on special knowledge' (1983, p.13). His analysis of this crisis identified, as one of the causes, a disjunction between the kinds of knowledge valued by academics and university-based researchers and those kinds of knowledge required by professionals in their everyday practice. Schön declared 'that professional knowledge is mismatched to the changing character of the situations of practice – the complexity, uncertainty, instability, uniqueness and value conflicts which are perceived as central to the world of professional practice' (1983, p.14). His generalization drew on the analyses by many leading professionals in various fields of the relevance of their professional knowledge bases to practice.

Schön was convinced that universities were committed to a view of knowledge 'that fosters selective inattention to practical competence and professional artistry' (1983, p.vii). The kinds of knowledge generated by researchers and academics did not, in his view, provide answers to the everyday problems confronted by practitioners because the problems of practice were different from the problems addressed by research. Indeed, the problems arising in practice, he claimed, were often not known to academics and researchers, and were not predictable either, because the situations in which practical problems arose were themselves characterized by unique events and therefore by uncertainty as well as instability and complexity. Hence, 'even if professional knowledge were to catch up with the new demands of professional practice,' he argued, 'the improvements in professional performance would only be transitory' (1983, p.15), because the problems of practice are never constant but are for ever evolving into new forms.

Case for a new epistemology

For Schön, the solution to this enduring problem, as indicated earlier, was to make a case for a new epistemology of practice which would acknowledge, and be based on, the ways of knowing of competent practitioners. Out of this came his ringing appeal for professionals to become reflective practitioners. Such an epistemology would validate the right of, and empower, practitioners to define their own problems of practice and to construct and regularly refine or reconstruct their own responses to those specific, challenging personal problems. The particular potential advantages of responses fabricated, and then refined, by practitioners would be their potency and their relevance to the individual practitioner and the unique work situation in which the problem arose. Such responses or solutions would reflect real-world problems and the knowledge, perspectives or frames of reference and ways of knowing of practitioners.

Of course, the outcomes of engaging in reflective practice have much broader ramifications than just those related to the professional practice of individuals. As Schön pointed out, the idea of reflective practice also has implications for, at least, practitioner-client relations, the organization in which the practitioner works, interactions between research and practice and between researcher and practitioner, and for the place of professions within the wider society. Some of these implications will be referred to in subsequent sections of this chapter. For the time being, let us examine in some detail the notion of reflection.

The key to engaging in reflective practice is, of course, being able to reflect. To provide a reasonably comprehensive framework for beginning to understand what reflective practice involves, there will be coverage of the different kinds of reflection, the modes and levels of reflection, the processes of reflection, and methods for promoting it. However, it must be pointed out that there is no single, widely accepted definition of reflection. Several authors have noted that there is considerable variance in the use of the term (Copeland *et al.*, 1993) or that different conceptions of reflection exist (Clarke, 1995; Gore and Zeichner, 1991).

Reflection

Meaning of the term

A generic view of reflective practice in education is that it is 'essentially concerned with how educators make sense of the phenomena of experience that puzzle or perplex them' (Grimmett *et al.*, 1990, p.20). At a very general level, reflection involves the identification of problematic issues within one's work situation. But it doesn't stop at identification. It also involves the search for, and trialling of, solutions that yield improved outcomes for the clients of practitioners. There is, however, at least one problem with such a simple explanation. It is that readers could be mislead into thinking that reflection is just technical problem solving, that is, routinely solving given problems by selecting and applying the most appropriate solution from a given set of solutions.

Reflective practice as distinct from technical problem solving

Schön went to considerable lengths in his text to draw a clear distinction between reflective practice and technical problem solving. To start with, Schon points out, the real-world problems with which practitioners have to contend are not presented to them as givens. Real-world problems are often very complex, do not fit conventional categories of known problems and have to be delineated or constructed by the practitioner from features in the problematic situation which, at first, may make little sense. Moreover, the practitioner also has to establish what constitutes acceptable ends and means for solving the problem. Once the problem has been set and the practitioner has framed the context in which the problem will be attended to, then attention can be given to planning and conducting experiments to solve the problem. However, the practitioner has to remain open to feedback from the experiment and may need to reframe the problem and define new ends and means for inquiry. As Clarke (1995) points out, practitioners 'come to new understandings of situations and new possibilities for action through a spiralling process of framing and reframing' (p.245). This requires the practitioner to keep conversing with the situation and remain attentive to what the situation feeds back by way of data on outcomes of the experiment.

Kinds of reflection

Schön identified two main kinds of reflection: reflection-in-action, which is thinking about what we are doing while we are doing it; and reflection-on-action, which involves retrospective deliberation about what we have done. He also made brief mention of a third kind of reflection: reflection on reflection. The focus of his 1983 publication, however, was on the distinctive structure of reflection-in-action whereas, in the decade and a half since his book, the notion of reflective practice that has been incorporated into numerous teacher education programmes is reflection-on-action. As Copeland *et al.* (1993) have reported, the literature on teacher education is 'replete with accounts of the reported success of reflective practitioners in changing and improving their own teaching... [and] of teacher education programmes instilling reflective "practices" in their students' (p.347).

Levels of reflection

From the foregoing, the inference could be drawn that reflection is a process which involves high level thought. By and large, that inference is a correct one. Francis (1995) is one who believes that 'reflection is more intellectually challenging than is generally recognized and that too little assistance is provided to teachers to help them observe, think through, reconstruct, and deeply understand the process of personal theory building' (p.229). This position appears to have general acceptance. At the same time, while not disputing the intellectual challenge associated with reflection, some authors have pointed out that reflection can occur at different levels. Three levels of reflection were identified by van Manen (1977).

The first is the technical level at which teacher reflections are focused on how best to accomplish a certain goal or whether teaching performance meets certain well-established criteria. There is no questioning of the appropriateness of the goals or criteria, just a concern with the efficiency and effectiveness of the means for attaining them. For example, a distance teacher may be concerned about whether adequate time was allocated in tele-tutorials to allow students to raise, and get assistance with, any problems they were encountering in the course. Another might wish to reflect on whether sufficient phone contacts with students were made to ensure that student motivation was maintained and that student attrition did not exceed an institutionally specified level.

The second level has been labelled the level of interpretative understanding (Copeland et al., 1993) or the practical level (Zeichner and Liston, 1987). At this level, teachers would be reflecting on the appropriateness or effectiveness of their actions and also on the adequacy of the goals towards which their actions were directed. There would be explication and clarification of the assumptions underlying their actions as well as consideration of the appropriateness of their actions and the goals they have adopted. For example, a distance educator might question whether there was too little or too much emphasis in assessment criteria on the requirement that students display critical thinking and whether the inclusion of critical thinking criteria was justifiable at all, given the level of the course or the absence in course materials of any explanation of critical thinking.

At the third level, referred to as the critical level, reflection involves a questioning of not just teacher actions and effects and the assumptions underlying action, but also the institutional contexts in which education is offered and even whether education is serving moral and ethical purposes. At this level, 'the major concern is with whether educational goals, activities, and experiences lead toward ways of living that are characterised by justice, equity, caring and compassion' (Gore and Zeichner, 1991, pp.122–3).

Reference to levels of reflection might convey the impression that the nurturance of reflective capacity should be progressive and that teachers should start reflecting at the technical level before moving to the other, so-called higher levels. This view is strenuously rejected by some (eg, Gore and Zeichner, 1991) who propose that teacher reflection across all three levels should be promoted, even with pre-service or beginning teachers. Gore and Zeichner contend that a developmental perspective, which implies that a critical level of reflection can be engaged only after first technical and then practical levels of reflection have been mastered, devalues both the technical skills of teaching and the teacher. They reject the view 'that the "critical" is somehow separate from the "technical" and "practical" classroom-based reality of student teachers, and that when broaching the critical, teacher educators are necessarily violating alleged "laws" of student teacher development. In our experience', say Gore and Zeichner, 'the "critical" is embedded in the very essence of the student teacher's classroom reality' (1991, pp.124–5). At the same time, they acknowledge that there is a problem in getting student teachers to see the links between technical and practical issues of the classroom and social, political and moral agendas.

A way of helping the reader clarify the different levels of reflection, based on the way research knowledge on teaching is used in reflective practice, has been offered by Grimmett *et al.* (1990). They have suggested that research knowledge can be used in reflective practice to direct practice; inform practice; and transform practice. There is a rough parallel here between this way of categorizing reflective practice and the three levels of reflection noted earlier – technical, practical and critical.

Processes of reflection

We shall look first at the structure of reflection-in-action as proposed by Schön (1983). His statements on the structure of this kind of reflection indicate the nature of the processes involved, as well as the order in which the processes occur. In the segment below, the structure has been outlined in list form. This may oversimplify the basic material or not do full justice to it and so, for these reasons, the reader is encouraged to check with Schön's original text. Schön's structure of reflection-in-action is represented as follows:

- A problematic issue is identified by a practitioner/inquirer.
- The issue is framed, by the inquirer, as a problem of design or understanding.
- Other phenomena in the practical setting are perceived (NB: Openness to the possibility of phenomena being incongruent with the initial framing of the problem is important.)
- The problem is reframed in the light of new phenomena. Inquirer draws on an element in personal repertoire to use as exemplar of, or metaphor for, new phenomena. On the basis of similarities perceived, new hypotheses are formulated.
- Inquiry turns into a frame experiment. Inquirer tests hypotheses by experimental actions which function to shape the situation and as probes for exploring it.
- Inquirer reflects on consequences of experiment (ie, attempts to shape the practical situation in line with initial frame).
- Inquirer frames new questions and new goals.

An example of reflection-in-action

The following example may help elucidate the nature of reflection-in-action. Let's suppose that Ben, a distance teacher at the tertiary level, is in the process of marking a batch of students' assignments. He notices that a large proportion of the students are failing and begins to feel concern. Ben decides to investigate the reason for the failure and, on the basis of an initial scan of the assignments he has marked, considers that the high failure rate might be due to the papers he has marked coming from an unrepresentative sample of less able students. As he continues to mark the assignments, the failure rate does not decline and he begins to discount his first tentative explanation. He begins to formulate and test other hypotheses –

that his assessment criteria are unrealistic, that insufficient instructional time was allocated to the topic, that the assignment topic was ill-defined, that his treatment of the topic was inadequate, that the students enrolled in his subject generally lacked ability, and so on. He frames and reframes the problem as he tests each of these hypotheses in turn by conferring with colleagues, checking the prior academic records of students, reviewing instructional materials, discussing his concerns with tutors and so on, but finds no evidence that would uphold any of the hypotheses he has explored thus far.

He now decides to review student written feedback on the subject that they have been submitting as they completed various modules and to talk to students about their perceptions of the subject and the way it was taught. Ben discovers that some of the students had disregarded or misread the advice about recommended prior studies in the area. Further checks confirm that the majority of students had an inadequate knowledge background to undertake study of his subject. As an outcome of the inquiry and reflection on what action to take, Ben decided to confer with affected students about the problem and to offer the option of additional make-up study and assessment. In addition, he decided to rewrite advice about prerequisites for entry to his subject.

This is a brief and rather sanitized outline of a distance educator reflecting-in-action. It lacks the detail and richness of information which is normally part and parcel of reflective practice. For fuller accounts of reflection-in-action, the reader is advised to check those provided by Schön in, for example, his vignettes of an architect, a psychotherapist, an engineer, a planner and a manager reflecting in their work situations (Schön, 1983) and also in his 1991 publication.

Reflective practice – an operational definition

To further elaborate descriptions of reflective practice, we turn now to an operational definition of reflective practice in teaching. Such a definition was assembled by Copeland *et al.* (1993) from an extensive review of the literature on reflection and interviews with educators. Their definition of this term includes 12 'critical attributes' (p.150) which are centred round four phases in the reflective process: identification of a problem; solution generation; solution testing; and learning from the process of reflection. The 12 critical attributes have been collapsed into the following set of five statements under the four phases:

Problem identification
- The problem which is to become the focus of reflective inquiry must be based on a practical or work situation, meaningful to the practitioner and relevant to success in teaching and learning.

Solution generation
- Possible solutions are to be formulated by the teacher and sourced in the teacher's own knowledge, including his or her own practical knowledge or understandings of research knowledge, for example.

- Consideration of solutions should lead to critical scrutiny of the teacher's actions and to possible positive effects on student learning.

Solution testing
- Each solution should be given a conceptual or mind test, then implemented, and its impact on teaching and learning assessed.

Learning from reflection
- Outcomes for the teacher should be reflected in changes to his or her practical theory, that is to beliefs, values, tactics, principles, interpretations of context or any of the other elements of his or her practical theory, singly or in combination.

In the first place, it should be noted that this definition is of what is taken to be a generic concept of 'reflective practice' because it is not clear from the article whether this conceptualization of reflective practice applies to reflection-in-action or reflection-on-action or both. Second, though multiple definitions do exist, many of them are variations of the above. As an example, consider the following synopsis of the reflective process from Ross (1990):

> The elements... include (not necessarily in this order):
> - Recognizing educational dilemmas;
> - Responding to a dilemma by recognizing both the similarities to other situations and the unique qualities of the particular situation;
> - Framing and reframing the dilemma;
> - Experimenting with the dilemma to discover the implications of various solutions;
> - Examining the intended and unintended consequences of an implemented solution and evaluating it by determining whether the consequences are desirable (p.98).

The above segment has treated the processes of reflection very broadly. There are many more aspects of reflective practice which, for space considerations, will not be covered here. Some will be taken up in subsequent sections of this chapter but the reader may also wish to pursue these independently, in which case reference to the work of Handal and Lauvas (1987), Calderhead (1989), Schön (1991), Grimmett and Erickson (1988) and Tabachnick and Zeichner (1991) would prove a useful starting point.

Reflection and critical thinking

Another useful concept for gaining insight into what is involved in the review and revision of personal practical theories is that of critical thinking. Much has been written about critical thinking; whole books have been devoted to its meaning and application. This suggests that the concept of critical thinking is a complex one, and indeed it is. Paul (1992), for example, posits that critical thinking has 35 dimensions. No attempt will be made here to provide a detailed analysis of the concept. Instead, after a few brief comments about the relationship between reflection and critical thinking, the focus will shift to some key components of critical thinking which add an important new dimension to ways of approaching the review and revision of practical theories.

A look at how some authors conceptualize critical thinking shows a degree of overlap between critical thinking and reflection. Brookfield (1991), for example, believes that critical thinking 'involves a reflective dimension' (p.14). Likewise, it could be argued, reflection involves critical thinking. Brookfield, however, takes this notion of overlap a step further and suggests that what Schön calls reflection in action is in fact 'critical thinking at the workplace' (p.155). Readers should be aware, then, that in some conceptual analyses no clear distinction is drawn between reflection and critical thinking; the two concepts are seen as at least somewhat complementary.

The extent of overlap between these two concepts will not be pursued further in these pages. Instead, some of the key processes in critical thinking which are often highlighted in the literature on this concept, and which differentiate it from other concepts, will be identified. These key processes will add an extra dimension to what has already been written about ways and means of reviewing and revising practical theories. Those key processes are exposed in this outline of how critical thinkers operate by Paul (1992):

> Critical thinkers use critical skills and insights to reveal and eradicate beliefs to which they cannot rationally assent. In formulating new beliefs, critical thinkers do not passively accept the beliefs of others; rather, they analyze issues themselves, reject unjustified authorities, and recognize the contributions of justified authorities. They thoughtfully form principles of thought and action; they do not mindlessly accept those presented to them (p.400).

This extract indicates what is a common core in most understandings of critical thinking. This core emerges again in the two activities that Brookfield (1991) rates as central to critical thinking: '(1) identifying and challenging assumptions and (2) exploring and imagining alternatives' (p.15). Hence, critical thinking is more than logical reasoning, trying to uncover fallacious argument or pointing out the flaws and other inconsistencies in the work of others. In addition to identifying and scrutinizing the assumptions on which beliefs and practices are based, critical thinking also involves constructing new visions and new scenarios, identifying the best alternative beliefs and practices, formulating justifications for these and establishing the soundness or rationality of those justifications. As Brookfield (1991) points out, 'critical thinking is a productive and positive activity' (p.5). So, the notion of critical thinking encourages a questioning of conventions, traditional practices and the taken-for-granted, rather than focusing on concerns, problems and discrepant events, as recommended by advocates of reflective practice. Thus a critical thinking approach to reviewing practical theories offers a different starting point – an examination of the assumptions underlying relatively standard practices which appear unproblematic. These might, in some contexts, include such practices as offering distance courses only within the framework of the normal academic year; providing supplementary readings only in printed form; and basing student assessment on lecturer or tutor ratings (and excluding self- or peer ratings).

Approaches to promoting reflection

Few would contest the view that most teachers are naturally reflective, at least some of the time. Problems arise in practice which cause teachers to ponder on why the problems occurred and what they could do to prevent the recurrence of the problems or to mitigate against their impact on classroom participants. However, this natural, tacit process of thinking about teaching often lacks the regularity, intensity of focus and rigour of the formalized versions of reflective practice. Finding ways of promoting systematic, rigorous reflection by teachers has exercised the minds of many interested in improving learning and teaching. A variety of approaches to promoting reflectivity have been trialled. Among these are autobiographies (Elbaz, 1988), ethnographic techniques (Gitlin and Teitelbaum, 1983), journal writing (Francis, 1995; Zeichner and Liston, 1987), the use of metaphors (Marshall, 1990; Ritchie and Russell, 1991; Tobin, 1990), and action research (Gore and Zeichner, 1991; Ross, 1989). Three of these approaches have been selected for more detailed comment below, because of their potential relevance to distance teachers wishing to review and revise their practical theories.

Journal Writing

Keeping a journal involves making daily or frequent and regular entries about experiences in teaching and then raising questions and concerns about those experiences. These records can then become the focus of reflection at that time or of further reflection later. According to those who have used this technique (eg, Zeichner and Liston, 1987), journal keeping does assist reflection and contribute to the critical analysis of teaching, but there are indications that the effects are more pronounced where two other conditions are met. The first condition is that, prior to the start of journal keeping, techniques for encouraging reflection be made explicit to the journal keeper. This recommendation is endorsed by Francis (1995) who found that, with her pre-service teachers, a framework based on Smyth's (1989) approach to personal and professional empowerment worked well. The framework they were advised to use consisted of four questions:

- What do I do as a teacher?
- What do the patterns of actions mean in terms of principles and beliefs underpinning action?
- How did I come to be this way?
- What other perspective could I adopt and what would I do differently as a result?

Practical theories of teaching: review and revision

Francis suggests that answering these questions takes the journal keeper through the four steps of description, analysis of information, confrontation and reconstruction, steps which roughly parallel the processes of reflection described earlier.

The second condition is that the journal keeper enters into a dialogue with a colleague or supervisor about the journal entries. The rationale for this is that feedback from another individual or team on the journal entries extends and enriches reflection by offering new perspectives on, and solutions to, problems and a fuller and more rigorous inquiry. The dialogue could take an oral or written form, with discussion also being facilitated via meetings or e-mail.

Clark and Peterson (1986) noted that the most extensive use of journal keeping had been made in the study of planning or instructional design, with teachers being asked to,

> keep a written record of their plans for instruction as they develop, and to comment in writing on (a) the context in which their plans are made, (b) their reasons for selecting one course of action over another, and (c) their reflections on and evaluation of their plans after they are brought into action in the classroom. (p.259)

The relevance of this to the distance teacher could hardly be plainer, especially when it is recalled that Schön (1983, 1987) believed that design is at the heart of all professional practice. Certainly, design is fundamental to all education. What all professional teachers do is supplant, or progressively refine, the instructional designs they create for the contexts in which they work, with new or better designs.

In summary, journal writing appears to offer a way of encouraging and facilitating teacher reflection.

Use of Metaphors

It has been noted that people often describe what they do in metaphorical terms (Lakoff and Johnson, 1980). They use metaphors to represent to themselves and to others their understandings of how they carry out their work. This certainly applies to teachers who have used numerous metaphors to reveal how they mentally structure their approach to their work and the roles they live out as teachers. It has been noted, for example, that some teachers depict themselves in the teaching role as cooks, coaches, gardeners, gate-keepers, entertainers and police (Jackson, 1968).

The suggestion has been made that perhaps metaphors could be used as a heuristic device to assist teachers to reconceptualize what they do and so improve teaching and learning (Tiberius, 1986; Tobin, 1990). Tobin suggested that metaphors might be used as 'master switches' to change beliefs and practices. The same point was made by Marshall (1990). She argued that, if we become cognisant of the metaphors that guide our thinking and action, we may be able to identify both those metaphors that do not match the problematic situations we are trying to resolve and those metaphors that result in unproductive actions. Furthermore, if we are able to restructure the frame through which we perceive a problem by generating alternative metaphors, we may be able to discover new perspectives and new solutions to problems. (p.128)

Until recently, the value of using metaphors as devices for changing how teachers taught had been largely untested. A case study reported by Tobin (1990) indicated that a teacher who had discarded his 'entertainer' and 'captain of the ship' metaphors for a perspective of himself as a 'gardener' effected some change in his teaching processes and became more nurturant in his interactions with students. A similar success story was told by Ritchie and Russell (1991). Russell was the teacher in their research project who adopted a new metaphor. She had expressed dissatisfaction with her teacher-centred approach to teaching junior science, the dissatisfaction being sourced in both student outcomes and her own self-assessment. As a result, she had become committed to using a constructivist approach and so developed a 'teacher as travel agent' metaphor to assist her to conceptualize and make the transition. The many parallels between travel agents and teachers with a constructivist orientation, outlined in their article, are compelling ones. Russell used the metaphor to make her classroom more like a travel agent's office with posters and brochures to inveigle students into taking intellectual trips. She planned individual excursions in science for individual students or groups of students to suit their own backgrounds, interests and needs. She redefined her role and that of her students. As a travel agent/teacher, she spent much less time in giving information to the whole class and planning class lessons and more time advising, interacting with groups, arranging student access to resources at appropriate times and serving as a tour guide. Moreover, she encouraged students to participate in their own tour/topic planning and to 'explore new routes as well as visiting well known destinations' (p.284) and, where they were able, to serve as tour guides themselves.

The transition was not without its problems but using the metaphor helped considerably. The authors claimed that using the metaphor contributed to changes in lesson planning, assessment techniques and maintenance of a constructivist approach across lessons. They also claimed that it gave students more knowledge of science and of their own strengths and weaknesses in the subject. Moreover, Russell also found the metaphor useful in resolving some of the problems that arose, such as those related to assessment, student concerns about assessment and her concerns about the quality of student thinking and questioning.

In the Ritchie and Russell case study, one of the major benefits of using metaphors as master switches is revealed. Their single metaphor provided a framework for working towards large-scale change. Furthermore, it allowed a coordinated attention to a wide range of elements in the teacher's practical theory and thus overcame the problem of small-scale, piecemeal change. It can be seen from their report that the elements of Russell's practical theory that were subjected to coordinated change covered roles of teacher and students, assessment, planning, contextual factors such as resources, beliefs, values, goals and management. Finally, frequent reference to, and reflection on, the metaphor, prior to and during the implementation phase, provided a basis for coherence in decision making.

Those who have used metaphors in programmes aimed at effecting change and improvement in teaching (Marshall, 1990; Ritchie and Russell, 1991; Tobin, 1990) have employed a number of different processes. When aggregated and sequenced, these include asking teachers to:

- list the roles they normally fulfil;
- identify the metaphors that underlie these roles and the ways they perform them;
- assess the appropriateness of these metaphors;
- generate alternative metaphors to provide new perspectives on their roles;
- test the appropriateness of these metaphors for potential use in teaching;
- design and implement new ways of teaching based on approved metaphors; and
- monitor the effects, evaluate and refine the practice of teaching and the metaphors on which it is based.

As can be seen, this sequence of processes offers numerous opportunities for reflection.

Action Research

The third approach to promoting reflection we shall look at is action research. This is a form of inquiry into practice which has surfaced at different places, in different ways and at different times. Not surprisingly, different streams of action research or different orientations to this form of inquiry have emerged (Cunningham, 1993). These have come, Cunningham points out, over the last 60 years from the contributions of people working in such fields as psychoanalysis, education, medicine, the armed forces, group dynamics and social anthropology. Perhaps, for this reason, there is no universally accepted definition of the term (Grundy and Kemmis, 1988).

Action research – the Deakin model

Because of the various forms and definitions of action research and the abundant literature associated with them, it is not possible to review them in this book. I have chosen, therefore, to focus on one, that developed by education staff at Deakin University in Australia and which I shall refer to as the Deakin model. Their approach to action research has played a significant part in professional development circles in education in Australia, and has won widespread acceptance and recognition overseas as well. The approach promulgated by the Deakin team has been developed and refined over many years and has been validated both practically and theoretically. It grows out of the same epistemological tradition as reflection and practical theory. All three invest power and responsibility in practitioners to improve the services they provide but, at the same time, to problematize their practice and the social context of teaching, to uncover and upgrade their practical theories and to improve the social and moral dimensions of communal life.

Action research – a definition

Kemmis and McTaggart, two of the main proponents of the Deakin model of action research, have defined it as:

> a form of collective self-reflective enquiry undertaken by participants in social situations in order to improve the rationality and justice of their own social or educational practices, as well as their understanding of these practices and the situations in which these practices are carried out. (1988, p.5)

Essential characteristics of action research

For practice-centred inquiry to be regarded as action research, a number of essential conditions must be met. First, action research is undertaken by a group seeking to make improvements to the individual work practices of group members in the interests of the clients they serve and to the culture of that group, but also to the wider society. Second, the desire for change must originate with the individuals. They must be motivated and committed to changing their practices and must own and direct the change process. Third, action research is a collaborative or group activity. It grows out of concerns shared by a group about their own individual practices and requires the involvement of all members of the group in the pursuit of improvements. Fourth, action research involves making improvements to practice by trying things out. Action research is, indeed, research on action and involves careful planning of new practices and monitoring of their effects. Inevitably, quality action research requires a high level of rigour but, at the same time, action researchers must be prepared for the unpredictable and therefore must be open and flexible.

Processes of action research

The basic pattern of action research has been represented in a diversity of ways. Stringer (1996), for example, has summarized it as a 'look-think-act' pattern which is repeated over and over while Kemmis and McTaggart (1988) represent action research as a spiral activity of planning, acting, observing and reflecting. Whichever abbreviated form is used to represent the pattern of activities, the basic processes are similar. A group engaged in action research begins by planning how their practices can be varied in response to a problem or concern that they have collectively identified and defined. The plan that emerges carries within it not just variations to practice but also the seeds for improvements to the group and the wider society. The plan then provides a basis and rationale for action (including how the consequences of actions will be monitored); however, alterations to plans must also be accommodated. Deviations from plans cannot be ruled out because of the inherent unpredictability of events and contexts in which human interactions occur. The group then acts out its plans both individually and collectively. During the implementation phase and afterwards, the third phase in the Kemmis and McTaggart spiral of activity, observation, is enacted. This involves the gathering and recording of evidence about the effects of the new actions and details of the action contexts. The evidence is used as the basis for reflection, the fourth phase, which can occur both during the implementation phase, to make changes to actions if these become necessary, and afterwards, before the next action phase. In summary, then, to do action research a group and its members undertake:

- to develop a plan of critically informed action to improve what is already happening.
- to act to implement the plan.
- to observe the effects of the critically informed action in the context in which it occurs, and
- to reflect on these effects as a basis for further planning, subsequent critically informed action and so on, through a succession of cycles. (Kemmis and McTaggart, 1988, p.10)

These brief accounts of the action research cycle hide its complexity and subtleties so, before embarking on any action research, readers are encouraged to tap the rich vein of material on the practicalities of this form of research which appear in the references.

Conclusion

The point was made at the start of this chapter that the purpose it was to serve was to make readers aware of what the review and revision of practical theories involves and to provide them with some basic insights into approaches to select from in undertaking this challenging but rewarding task.

Invitation to Reflect

You are now invited to reflect on what you have read in this chapter and to begin to develop an approach to reviewing and revising your own practical theory of distance teaching. As you can see, the review and revision task is a complex one and will consume much time and intellectual energy.

Here are some suggestions about formulating your approach.

- Take your time. Don't rush in and make premature commitments to an approach that you will be unable to sustain.
- Take stock of your own situation. Make a careful reconnaissance of such features of your work context as:
  - what is known about the effectiveness of your distance teaching materials and approach;
  - time available;
  - institutional policy on design of distance education subjects;
  - factors likely to constrain or facilitate review and revision of practical theory and practice; and
  - resources that are readily accessible.
- Start small. Try to ensure that what you set out to do initially is achievable.
- Formulate a tentative approach. If it involves a team, ensure that the approach has been carefully negotiated and has the commitment of others.

Chapter 4

Review and revision of practical theories of distance teaching: some issues for consideration

Review In the first two chapters, you were introduced to the notion of practical theories and to the elements, structure and significance of such theories. One of the reasons given for the significance of practical theories was that practical theories are the main determinants of what teachers do in practice and therefore of the quality of their professional work. It was argued that change and improvement in teaching performance requires the review and revision, by individual teachers, of their own practical theories. This involves a progressive reconstitution of the frameworks through which they view classrooms and define their roles. This process of review and revision must start with a clear and comprehensive appreciation of existing frameworks or theories. A first step, then, for distance teachers, involves becoming aware of your own personal theories of distance teaching. Once your theory has been made explicit, then it can more easily be subjected to critical scrutiny and, if necessary, revision.

The review and revision of practical theories was the focus of Chapter 3 where various approaches to this challenging task were outlined. Towards the end of Chapter 3, you were encouraged to give thought to how you might go about the review of your own practical theory and to formulate a plan for doing so.

> ## Focus of Chapter
>
> This chapter and the next have been designed to assist you with the review and revision of your practical theory of distance teaching. To this end, some of the major issues and trends in distance education today will be explored and some possible responses will be outlined. This material has been provided to illustrate the kinds of themes which might be the subject of your own review and revision process. In no way is it meant to prescribe what should be the focus of your own reflections or how you should respond to those matters.

Issue 1: Open Learning in Distance Education

The trend to open learning

Over the last decade, open learning has become established as a very clear educational trend. Open learning provisions are now commonplace in institutions offering programmes at compulsory, post-compulsory and higher levels of education as well as in businesses, industries and social service agencies. Materials which offer open learning opportunities are now commonly dispensed via distance education programmes. The rapid spread of the open learning concept has been attributed to the advent of new technologies and to a pervasive and enduring turbulence in economic, commercial, social and political spheres. This turbulence has given rise to an appreciation of the need for widespread and rapid reforms, reforms which require not just changes to practices but also changes to the mindsets which shape work practices. For the reforms to succeed, a basic requirement is a re-educated and a better educated workforce. Part and parcel of this demand for reform has been a heightened sensitivity to the need for education and subsequently to the needs, prior learning, dispositions and environments for study of learners, and a greater emphasis on access and equity in educational provisions. Having noted the trend to open learning, let us first examine what open learning is and what it does before scrutinizing its implications for the way we teach in distance education.

Open education and open learning

The concept of open learning is, to some extent, another manifestation of a form of educational progressivism which surfaced most recently in the 1960s and 1970s and was known then as the open education movement. In that era, the major impact was on education in the compulsory years. As the title implies, the aim of the movement was to open up or free up education by giving students a much greater role in decisions about what they would learn and how, when, where and with whom. Open education has been conceptualized in a variety of ways, as 'a set of teacher attitudes and beliefs about children and learning… as open space, multi-age grouping and team teaching…[and] as individualising instruction, or pupils' behaviours, such as setting their own goals' (Giaconia, 1987, p.247). Proponents of the movement also advocated a new, open-space style of architecture for schools and classrooms which would be more facilitative of the methods of open education. Needless to say, occupancy of an open-design classroom did not oblige teachers to use open methods; likewise open methods were sometimes practised by teachers who occupied conventional classroom spaces.

The general understanding of open education methods within the educational community was, as Horwitz (1979) noted, that they involved flexible use of space, student choice of activity, richness of learning materials, and more individual and small-group learning activities than whole-class instruction. The basic principle which underpinned open education, however, was that of optimizing or at least extending student choice.

The meaning of open learning

That same principle of optimizing student choice underpins the notion of open learning. Though a definition of the term is somewhat difficult to pin down (Bosworth, 1991) because of diverse interpretations, most would agree to start with that open learning opportunities provide students with 'as much choice and control as possible over course content, learning strategies and learning resources' (Foks, 1988, p.7). Of course, there are many more facets to the concept of open learning. Other aspects of learning programmes which can be opened up or made more flexible include student access to learning programmes, assessment practices, modes of delivery, and time and place of study. One definition which touches on many facets of the concept describes open learning as:

> an approach rather than a system or technique; it is based on the needs of individual learners, not the interests of the teacher or the institution; it gives students as much control as possible over what and when and where and how they learn; it commonly uses the delivery methods of distance education and the facilities of educational technology; [and] it changes the role of a teacher from a source of knowledge to a manager of learning and a facilitator. (Johnson, 1990, p.4)

Reasons for advocating open learning

Advocates of open learning have pushed the adoption of this mode because they argue that it more fully caters for human diversity in learning needs, goals, styles and contexts. An open learning approach can accommodate such diversity because it allows learners to negotiate personally relevant goals and then to follow individual learning pathways and timeframes to achieve those goals. Advocates believe that, if education provisions are to assist people to realize their full potential, then diversity in the ways that learning programmes are structured is essential. Their promotion of open learning reflects a keen dissatisfaction with conventional education: in their view, traditional education overlooks the different needs and learning styles of students. Moreover, they would argue that giving students a greater say in matters relating to their own learning encourages student independence and autonomy. All of this means that students play a more active role in their own learning which, in turn, empowers them and increases the potency and relevance of their own learning.

Support for open learning also derives from concerns about social equity. As Thorpe and Grugeon (1987) noted, closed approaches to learning give greater priority to institutional needs than those of learners and make provisions which suit 'only a small sub-set of the potential learner population' (p.4). Organizations committed to open learning will seek to widen access to educational opportunities so that those with potential are not barred from entry on the grounds of, for example, work conditions which prevent attendance at scheduled classes; remoteness from campus; physical disability; absence of formal credentials or a non-traditional educational background. The goal of such learning organizations is to have admission policies which are inclusive rather than exclusive and which extend rather than restrict categories for admission.

A third impetus towards open learning has come from recent reformations in the spheres of industry and commerce. Over the last decade or so, there has been an urgent and rapidly escalating need for business and industry to reorient and restructure. This need has arisen from challenges posed by global competition, threats to corporate profitability and viability, rising expectations about the quality of products and services, new technologies, new levels of accountability and a host of other factors. What has made this need such a critical one, and the finding of a response such a compelling and urgent one, is the magnitude of the challenges and the serious consequences of ignoring them. What has exacerbated the situation even more is the rapidity with which these challenges have accumulated.

Meeting this need involves a rapid re-education and retraining of the workforce. Moreover, in order to cope with fast-paced change, the processes of re-education and retraining have become an essential and fixed feature of the workplace. These new circumstances brought with them a need for considerable flexibility and diversity in the provision of learning services. Providers of learning services had to be responsive to the specific requirements of different organizations and differences among learners in respect of when and for how long they could study, styles of learning, prior learning, pacing, need for learning support, suitable venues for learning and certification requirements. Such requirements made a high level of openness an essential attribute of the learning system. Writing in 1990, Johnson concluded that open learning would be 'the only way to cope' (p.12) with the demand in Australia for retraining arising from government policies and award restructuring. In similar vein, Thorpe and Grugeon (1987) had noted a trend in British industry in the mid-1980s towards the use of open learning as a means of meeting the training needs of industry. Finally, it should be noted that the staff development reforms within business and industry outlined above were not just passively noted by governments; they were actively supported and, in many cases, promulgated by governments because of the perceived nexus between national prosperity and revitalized business and industrial sectors.

Research on open learning

A computer-aided search of recent research literature on open learning in post-compulsory and higher education contexts identified scores of articles and monographs which display a diversity of interests and issues. For example, reports document the use of open learning in different places (Lewis, 1995; Wade and Sutton, 1994), technologies that support open learning (Oliver and Grant, 1994), the impact of an open learning initiative on people with disabilities (Walker, 1994), potential problems with the use of open learning (George, 1995) and the integration of open learning and distance education (Maxwell, 1995) .

Collectively and individually, these and similar pieces make a useful contribution to the literature on open learning. Some would undoubtedly help readers towards a decision about the adoption of open learning approaches; however, it would appear from this limited review that research evidence on any specific issue related to open learning at post-compulsory and higher levels of education has not reached anything like critical mass. Currently, there is insufficient evidence to confirm the alleged benefits of open learning approaches in further and higher education institutions. However, this should not deter readers from considering extending their use of open approaches. Issues that require attention have sometimes to be resolved on moral or ethical grounds alone. Moreover, innovations to practice need not necessarily be delayed, awaiting a verdict from traditional research studies, when action research represents a viable option.

Nevertheless the extensive research on open education in primary and secondary schools may give some grounds for confidence in open learning approaches and encouragement to would-be innovators to proceed. In a review of meta-analyses of the outcomes of school programmes in both open and formal settings, involving well over 200 studies, Giaconia (1987) concluded that:

> in general, open education is somewhat more effective than traditional education for nonachievement outcomes (such as cooperativeness, self-concept, attitude to teacher, creativity and independence) [and that] traditional education is only slightly more effective than open education for the traditional academic achievement measures. (p.250)

A rider was added by Giaconia to the effect that there were considerable variations in outcomes across open education settings.

So open education appears to offer mixed blessings for primary and secondary students. Now, of course, these conclusions cannot be generalized to all settings in which open education or open learning occurs. Varying the context in which the research is conducted could well produce a reversal of an earlier pattern of findings or some other significant change. In summary, then, research indicates that some of the alleged benefits of open education were in line with predictions in some settings. However, it falls well short of providing a categorical assurance that open education is always, in every situation, the best alternative.

Implications of Open Learning for Practical Theories of Distance Education

Obviously, open learning has implications for institutions which offer educational programmes as well as for their staff. There are not, however, two distinct sets of implications – one for the institution and one for the staff member – because any decision by the institution to move towards greater openness in learning has consequences for the staff member and vice versa. However, the following discussion of implications will be from the perspective of a staff member because the central focus in this book is on the personal practical theories of teachers, not some aggregated or consensual practical theory representing an institutional view of teaching.

A commitment to greater openness could require a reconsideration of many aspects of the subjects we teach. Here are some of those aspects along with some suggested lines of inquiry.

Admission requirements

Given the need for more open access, consideration could be given to admitting a more diverse student group. For example, a subject on teaching effectiveness may have been designed for primary and secondary teachers, but the list of potential students of such a subject need not be so tightly circumscribed. With suitable modification, the subject could also attract those who teach in pre-schools, kindergartens, nurse education programmes and tertiary institutions generally and those involved in industry training.

> Should the student group be extended?
> What are the consequences for other elements of the subject?
> Should entry requirements be changed to admit those who lack formal qualifications?

These are just some of the questions that could be pursued.

Content of the subject

Since the academic or professional needs of students could be very diverse and therefore not met fully by a fixed body of content, the desirability of allowing for content options could be considered. The issue that arises concerns the extent to which the content for study should be specified. There are a number of positions that could be taken including that:

1. students should be required to complete core studies and allowed some elective study;
2. they be allowed to specify those topics they wish to study from an educational menu;
3. all content should be specified by the teacher or curriculum guide; and
4. no content be specified and that students be allowed to define their own content for study.

Obviously, any decision will need to take account of the nature of the course in which the subject is embedded, certification requirements, if any, and the needs and backgrounds of learners.

Teaching and learning strategies

The challenge here is to find ways of providing learning experiences which will cater for student diversity in learning styles, goals, needs and approaches. Formulating a response will require careful analysis of those likely to seek admission. A consideration of how, when, where and why students learn and their motives for study always proves a useful starting point. Thought could then be given to the kinds of learning activities in which students might be engaged and the methods, media and resources required to provide those opportunities for learning.

Options for promoting open learning in distance education are very extensive indeed and are well canvassed in many texts (see, for example, Bosworth, 1991; Lockwood, 1995; Rowntree, 1992). Learning activities, for example, can range across those involving individual study, group work, field work, learning-on-the-job, laboratory practicals, and interaction with computer-based resources and discussion. Methods can include direct instruction, role-plays and simulations, group investigations, teleconferencing, case study methods, personalized self-instruction and audio-visual presentations. A considerable variety of media and resources are also available to the distance teacher. These have been boosted in recent years by the development of extensive networks of information, held at Web-sites all over the globe, to which learners can gain access via computers.

Decisions about which open learning opportunities to provide are not easily made. They are governed to some extent by resources available to the institution and the staff member, by credentialling requirements and by the willingness or preparedness of learners to engage in open learning. These and other issues are discussed by Rowntree (1992) who concludes that a distance teacher should feel able to set (and I would add, provide justification for) their own limits: 'These are the learners to whom I can open new opportunities. These are the ways in which I will make learning more productive and satisfying for them. More than that I cannot do – as yet' (p.28).

Assessment

Making assessment practices more open could follow a number of pathways:

- varying assessable activities, by negotiation between teacher and learners, to suit the needs and interests of different learners;
- introducing a variety of assessment practices to include teacher assessment, peer assessment, self-assessment or some combination of these; and
- varying the submission dates or times at which learners present themselves for assessment, as in personalized self-instruction.

This last measure could have the effect of extending the duration of the subject, an arrangement which may not be acceptable to either the staff member or institution or both. As Johnson (1990) points out, however, 'open learning is not interested in how long the student takes to master the task but is vitally interested in the degree of mastery' (p.18).

A commitment to open learning also has implications for a variety of other, largely pedagogic matters, such as the role of the teacher, teacher-student relationships, contact time with students, arrangements for granting credit for prior learning, and when the subject will be offered and its duration. It should be obvious, then, that a move towards open learning could involve substantial adjustments to one's practical theory of teaching and make significant demands on time and energy. Nevertheless, despite the costs and the risks, there are some compelling arguments in favour of open learning with which you need to come to grips.

Invitation to Reflect

You are now invited to reflect on the extent of your own present commitment to open learning and whether change is necessary or desirable. Here are some of the broad questions you might consider:

- What open learning practices do you currently facilitate? Where would you place yourself on the closed learning – open learning continuum? Would your colleagues and students concur?
- What obstacles to open learning does your current approach to distance teaching present? Can these be justified? Has student feedback indicated a desire for greater openness in learning?
- Are there ways in which you could extend student choice and give them greater control over their own learning? What are the implications of such changes for you? For the course? For the institution in which you work?

Another way in which you might reflect on your own position in relation to open learning would be to examine details in components of the practical theory of a distance teacher who has a strong commitment to open learning. Some of those details are provided below. An attempt has been made to include details which are important. You may disagree with this list and wish to delete some or include others which you think deserve a higher priority. Feel free to vary the details but when you have compiled a set which, in your view, reflects more accurately a commitment to an open learning approach, then consider the extent to which you could internalize and accommodate them within your own practical theory of distance teaching. The details have been placed in groups according to the components of practical theories as presented earlier in Figure 2.1.

Distance teachers with a commitment to open learning are likely to:

- Value or attach great importance to: diversity in students, collaboration and negotiation with students on subject-related matters, individuality or uniqueness, flexibility and equity in education (*values*).
- Believe that: students are capable of directing and monitoring their own learning with appropriate support; open learning can empower students and enhance their self-esteem; open learning can give rise to greater improvements in the quality and potency of student learning; and open learning can lead to improved student attitudes to learning and teachers (*beliefs*).
- Promote student autonomy, independence; cater for diversity in ways students learn; and enhance student access to the subjects they teach (*goals*).
- Seek to induce in students: high levels of confidence in their ability to be self-directive in respect of learning; an internal locus of control; assertiveness; and reflectivity, including dispositions towards being introspective and self-analytical (*student states*).
- Take steps to: negotiate individual learning packages with students, including assessment tasks; provide a range of learning activities which students could use, select from or, in cooperation with the teacher, adapt or supplement; use a range of media as appropriate (eg, print, telephone, computer, satellite, and interactive multimedia); and identify a range of resources and/or resource locations (*strategies*).
- Draw to a greater extent on, or develop more fully, personal capacities for openness, flexibility, tolerance of diversity, negotiating, establishing rapport with students and ceding greater control to students (*teacher attributes*).
- Gather extensive data on the learning needs, styles, approaches, etc of distance students, the environments in which they work and study and other factors which could impinge on decisions about the openness of teaching and learning materials (*contextual variables*).
- Strive to: provide support for learners seeking to exploit open learning opportunities; monitor student progress frequently; individualize feedback to students; foster convivial interpersonal relationships which encourage students to engage in open learning; and vary the degree of open learning opportunities to suit individual needs (*principles*).

Issue 2: Knowledge of Students

An issue for reflection

What should distance teachers know about the student populations for whom they design courses and subjects and the specific groups of students who enrol in those courses and subjects? This has always been a critical issue because inadequate or inappropriate information about the students we teach could compromise the quality of the materials we design and the educational experiences we provide. For example, if we are not well informed about students' prior learning or educational backgrounds, the content prescribed for study may be too easy or too difficult, coverage of content may be too fast or too slow and the feedback we provide on student work may be too detailed or too vague to be helpful. The issue of what knowledge distance teachers should hold about students has assumed more prominence with the advent of open learning, because adoption of an open learning philosophy means that educational provisions must become learner-centred, with student learning needs given a top priority in educational decision making.

Invitation to Reflect

There are numerous questions we can ask ourselves about what we should know about the distance learners we teach. Here are some. Think carefully about your responses to each.

- What do I actually know about the students I teach and for whom I design distance materials? Is the information reliable and valid? Do I know enough about the students to provide opportunities for open learning?
- What assumptions have I made about distance students on which I have based my teaching? Are these assumptions sound ones? How can I check them out?
- What information about students do I need in order to be an effective designer and teacher of distance materials? How can I obtain this information?

We will begin to present material relevant to these questions for you to reflect on in a moment but first we should note the two sides to the issue of knowledge of students. For a distance teacher involved in both design of distance materials and teaching, two sets of knowledge of students are required. One set is required for the design phase, but teachers also need to know about students in a different kind of way when the materials are being used by students in a course of study.

Knowledge of students required for course design

Design of distance materials requires knowledge of many kinds – knowledge of curriculum, of pedagogy, of learners and the learning process, and subject matter knowledge, to name a few. Curriculum writers have had much to say on this issue. Their views are usually reflected, at least to some degree, in the knowledge dispensed in pre-service teacher education programmes. All are agreed, however, that knowledge of learners is critical to successful curriculum design. What is needed is knowledge about the general student population for whom the subject is being planned. The student population comprises all those who are likely to enrol in the subject over the life-span of the subject. For example, the student population might be all first-year students likely to enrol in an undergraduate engineering course over the next five years, or community members who may be interested in 'An introduction to computers' subject offered as a hobby class at a community college, or all students about to embark on their primary education at schools within an educational system.

Usually, the characteristics of a student population can be known only in a very general sense. Experienced junior secondary teachers, for example, have general knowledge about what Year 10 students will be like, knowledge which they have built up over many years of teaching experience with Year 10s. They know their general behaviour patterns, what interests them, what causes them embarrassment and what learning problems they encounter. Calderhead (1983) reported that experienced teachers had a general idea of what their new classes would be like, even before they met them. Hence knowledge of a student population is knowledge of a generic rather than specific kind. It is general knowledge about a particular sub-set of society, not detailed knowledge of the individual members of that sub-set. This general knowledge would usually include demographic knowledge about the student population, knowledge of patterns of human development for the particular age group, about prior educational studies, about theories of learning relevant to the student population and so on.

The kinds of knowledge about students needed for course or subject design purposes in distance education will depend on many factors – the nature of the subject, the course within which it is located, the learning goals and whether they involve skills or affect, perceptions of the teacher's role and that of students, the modes of delivery available within the teaching institution, the degree of openness in student learning that is to be encouraged, and the availability and location of learning resources. The discursive and research literatures therefore offer no prescriptive advice about the kinds of knowledge you should seek about students; they do provide suggestions from which you can draw. However, requirements will vary from subject to subject for the same teacher and from teacher to teacher.

There are some suggestions of the kinds of information that teachers may need. Harrison (1991) suggests that the following broad categories of knowledge about the target group of students may be helpful:

- knowledge of their attitudes to undertaking study, to various study approaches, to their work and to career development;
- knowledge of educational backgrounds of students in relation to their previous study experiences, level of post-compulsory education, and literacy and numeracy standards;
- knowledge of what motivates them;
- knowledge of what interests them at work and at leisure; and
- knowledge of impediments to learning such as health conditions, limited attention span, and what distracts learners.

Another set of categories, proposed by Rowntree (1992), overlaps with that proposed by Harrison to some extent. Rowntree proposed that distance teachers consider gathering data on the student population in relation to its:

- demographic factors – age, sex, race, occupations, personal handicaps, and places of residence;
- motivation – reasons for learning, work-study links, and benefits of study;
- learning factors – skills, styles, conceptions of learning, experiences of open learning;
- subject background – prior learning and experiences in the subject area and attitudes to the subject;
- resource factors – contexts for study, time for study and means of access to resources and to support.

Invitation to Reflect

Think about the kinds of knowledge you need about learners in order to make appropriate decisions regarding the design of distance teaching materials for the particular context in which you teach.

What do you need this knowledge for? Do you have the knowledge needed for:

- Choosing an appropriate writing style?
- Identifying what knowledge learners will start the subject with?
- Providing examples of concepts that will be meaningful to learners?
- Designing activities for learners to undertake that will assist understanding of content?

Which of the categories suggested by Harrison and Rowntree would be essential in your situation? How would you justify your choice? Do colleagues and potential students have alternative viewpoints? Which categories would be valuable but not essential?

Ways of acquiring knowledge of the population of learners

Thought also needs to be given to means of acquiring the knowledge needed for design purposes and ensuring that it provides a valid basis for decision making. The information could be gained via questionnaires mailed to a representative sample of potential students, a process made easier if potential students are already enrolled in other subjects offered by the institution. In this case, useful information may already be held by other teachers or the institution itself. An approach to agencies or associations which represent groups of potential students either industrially or professionally may also prove helpful. Such organizations may have researched the training or educational needs of their members and may therefore be able and willing to offer relevant data. Another common practice is to appoint representatives of the potential student group to the design team, with a brief to keep the design team informed of student perspectives, needs, interests, etc. as appropriate.

Knowledge of students required for teaching purposes

The second kind of knowledge of students that could prove very useful to distance teachers is knowledge of the students who actually enrol in the subject, year by year or semester by semester. This kind of knowledge is, of course, a knowledge of specifics; it includes knowledge of the particular class, of the groups of students within it and also knowledge of the individual student members of the class. This kind of knowledge might be described as somewhat clinical in nature because it comes from up-close contact with a class and one-on-one contact with individual students. It is therefore quite different from the earlier kind of knowledge of students, the kind required for design purposes. It is more fine-grained because it relates to one intake of students and to the individual members of that intake. Of course, any intake or sample of students can vary markedly, in terms of characteristics, from those of the student population so there could be substantial differences between group norms and population norms.

One of the first to indicate the pedagogical importance of this kind of teacher knowledge was Elbaz (1983) who described it as a kind of practical knowledge. This kind of teacher knowledge of students is not textbook knowledge; it is not found in books on human development and learning, educational psychology or special education. It is knowledge acquired by teachers through practice or experiences with learners, and serves practical purposes. As Kagan and Tippins (1991) point out, there has been little research into teachers' practical knowledge of students. What little there is has been reviewed by Kagan and Tippins and also by Mayer *et al.* (1994). Unfortunately, none of the research reviewed refers to teachers in distance education contexts. A careful assessment needs to be made, therefore, of whether the benefits of practical knowledge of students would apply also to distance teachers. Consider, then, the claims made for knowing students well, in respect of teachers who have face-to-face contact with students.

Value of knowledge of individual learners

The value of this kind of knowledge for optimizing the learning of individual students in conventional classrooms has been reported in a number of places (Anning, 1988; Marland, 1986; Mayer *et al.*, 1994; Phillips *et al.*, 1993). These studies indicate, for example, that knowing individual students well allows teachers to set appropriate expectations for them, to personalize their interactions with students, to bend rules where such leniency seems warranted and makes sense strategically, to constitute groups that will have some prospect of working effectively, to select respondents to questions and to make a host of other decisions relevant to the best interests of individual students, groups or the class as a whole. These studies support anecdotal reports from classroom teachers which point to knowledge of students being a key to effective teaching. Teachers in the study by Mayer *et al.* endorsed this view most emphatically, maintaining that, if they didn't have an in-depth knowledge of students, the educational provisions made for their students would undoubtedly fall below the best they could offer. A similar view was expressed by Phillips *et al.* (1993) following their study of outstanding teachers working in composite classes, that is, classes comprised of students normally placed in two grades. These authors concluded that 'one of the major reasons these teachers were outstanding was because they knew and understood each child so well and they used this knowledge to manage, correct and stimulate children's learning' (1993, p.15).

Does this proposition about the link between teaching effectiveness and knowledge of students apply to distance teaching? The answer we could expect to get from advocates of open learning would almost certainly be in the affirmative. For what it's worth, I also would support the proposition. Why? Because knowledge of individual students allows us to individualize or particularize provisions for each learner and so enhance opportunities for learning. Moreover, such knowledge eventually can sharpen perceptions about the strengths and weaknesses inherent in the distance education materials we prepare and use and point to ways of improving them. Here are some examples of the ways in which detailed knowledge of individual distance students can be used to good effect.

- Knowledge of a student's work context (many distance students are in full-time employment) may provide insights into the reasons for learning problems and orientation to study and provide a basis for choice of examples or terminology by the distance teacher in dialogue with the learner.
- Knowledge of a student's study environment could influence the distance teacher's advice about resources to use, reaction to late submission of work and suggestions about gaining access to support.
- Knowledge of a student's conception of learning may be reflected in the nature of feedback provided on assignment work, negotiations with the learner about goals and techniques in project work for assessment and advice on meta-cognitive strategies to be adopted.

Without such knowledge, the interactions between distance teacher and distance learner would be far less beneficial. They could not easily be customized by the distance teacher to suit the needs of the individual student.

What knowledge of distance students might be of worth?

What kinds of knowledge about students who actually enrol in a subject in any term or semester might be helpful to distance teachers? The answer to that would depend once again on the individual teacher and the specifics of the context in which the subject is being offered. The suggestions by Harrison (1991) and Rowntree (1992) referred to earlier should again provide useful starting points. It is also usually wise to provide opportunities for students to add other information that they consider may be of interest or relevance to the teacher. Remember that what is of interest now is the detail in the profile of each individual learner, not the norms and generalizations about students as a whole which could be derived from them. Nevertheless, these data can be used to check on the assumptions on which work in the design phase was based.

Ways of acquiring knowledge of individual learners

The next question to think about is how to acquire information on individual distance students. Enrolment forms which students have to complete to gain entry to a course or subject provide some useful knowledge about students such as place of residence, academic record, native language, nature and place of employment, ethnicity and any specific disabilities. Where additional data are required, these can be obtained by asking students to provide such information by e-mail or by completion and return of a student profile form. It is also worth noting that some distance teachers have adopted the practice of providing their students with relevant information about themselves. Contact with students via telephone, teleconferences or during orientation days at study centres provides yet other means of rounding out individual profiles.

> ### Invitation to Reflect
>
> Take some time now to reflect on the kinds of knowledge of individual students you currently use or might need as a distance teacher.
>
> - What kinds of knowledge do you currently hold?
> - How do you use that knowledge?
> - Is it used effectively? What data do you have on your use of it?
>
> What might you profitably add to your store of knowledge about individual students?
>
> - Can you justify these additions to yourself? To colleagues?
> - Might your distance students want to share with you some information about themselves which they consider it important for you to have?
> - How best could such knowledge be acquired?
> - What principles should be observed in the provision and storage of such information?
> - What are some effective ways of using that knowledge?

Extending Knowledge of Individual Students: Implications for Practical Theories of Distance Teaching

Any extension to a distance teacher's knowledge base about individual students represents a change to the 'contextual factors' component of that teacher's practical theory. That change, especially if it is a substantial one, is almost certainly going to have repercussions on other elements of the distance teacher's practical theory. A distance teacher contemplating the extension of his or her knowledge about individual students in order to make use of that additional data to improve the quality of teaching and learning, is contemplating change to practice and, *ipso facto*, to the theory that guides practice. For such a change to have the best chance of success, it is essential that the consequences of that decision for other components be fully identified and assessed. Many attempts at changing teaching have come to grief because of the failure to consider the ripple effects of change to one component on all the other components. It is important to recognize that teaching is a complex activity in which the relationships among components is an organic one.

Let us now consider some of the implications of a change to the knowledge base in respect of individual students for other components of a practical theory of distance teaching. In the first place, it is very probable that a decision to acquire and use extra knowledge about students reflects some change to basic beliefs and values. Such a change could be consistent with a greater commitment to open learning and therefore to the goals, beliefs and values which underpin that approach.

A second implication is that some new strategies may need to be adopted. It could mean, for example, that if this new knowledge is to provide scope for greater individualization of learning, that ways of negotiating learning contracts will have to be put in place, requiring more frequent contact between teacher and student.

Third, more frequent contact between teacher and student may expose the teacher to a greater range of student states than hitherto. Thus the formerly covert reactions of students become overt or explicit. The reforming distance teacher may become aware, for example, of the uncertainty that some students have about subject requirements or of the lack of confidence in their ability to cope with assessment demands. Student apprehension about, or rejection of, the new approach or frustration over time delays in negotiations might also surface. On the other hand, some students might react with delight and enthusiasm to the new opportunities and want to take initiatives that the distance teacher may consider too extreme or too demanding on time or other resources. In either case, strategies for dealing with these student states need to be considered and ready for use.

Fourth, new operating principles may be needed to ensure the success of the new strategies. For example, the distance teacher might need to adopt the principle of always responding positively and warmly to contacts initiated by the students so that a sense of trust between teacher and student can be developed. Finally, all of these changes may have implications for the range of personal attributes which the distance teacher may need to draw on to bolster or magnify the effects of the new strategies to be adopted. The proposed changes may require, on the part of the distance teacher, greater sensitivity to students' subtle expressions of need, or greater flexibility. Then the question arises: How will the distance teacher give expression to these attributes?

Invitation to Reflect

This is a follow-up to the previous Invitation to Reflect in which you were invited to consider whether, in the interests of better learning and teaching, you could or should extend your knowledge of individual students. The decision you took could not, of course, be taken without reference to your goals in teaching, your educational values and beliefs, the strategies you use and so on. Make sure, however, that you have thought through fully the implications of that decision about extending your knowledge of students for all components of your practical theory.

Issue 3: Student Interactivity

Student interaction with text

One of the concerns of distance teachers has been to find ways of encouraging students to interact with the content in distance materials, that is, to ask questions of it, to consider its application in their workplaces and to critique it rather than just reading it through in non-stop fashion. Ways of encouraging students to interact with the content in subjects taught at a distance has exercised the minds of many. Rowntree (1992), for example, developed the notion of a 'tutorial-in-print' as a way of getting students to think about what they were reading. He saw this device as simulating the dialogue between a student and tutor. This and other kinds of activities that frequently feature in self-instructional material, such as the reflective action guide and a dialogic approach, are fully dealt with in a book by Lockwood (1992).

Another dimension of interactivity

There is, of course, another dimension to student interactivity, and that has to do with interactions between a distance student and a distance teacher, or between a distance student and other students, colleagues, friends and other resource personnel. It is this dimension of student interactivity that is of special interest here. The issue to be explored in relation to student interactivity is whether, in the approach to distance teaching that has been adopted, a sufficient emphasis has been placed on student interaction with teachers, other students, colleagues and other resource personnel to ensure the best possible learning.

Rationale for student interaction with others

One of the features of modern, good quality classroom teaching at all levels is the rich diversity of patterns of interaction. During teaching and learning activities, students interact with teachers, lecturers, other students, principals, teacher-librarians, laboratory assistants, proctors, tutors and a range of other resource staff in a variety of settings, both formal and informal. Formal settings include role plays, simulations, group discussions, practical work, field studies and question-and-answer sessions. The basic reason for this commitment on the part of teachers to facilitating high levels of interaction and to a diversity of interaction patterns is that learning is seen as a social process, in part at least, and that discussion in social settings is a powerful medium for learning. Students learn through discussion. By interacting with others about the content of the subject, it is believed that students negotiate new understandings and develop changed perspectives on problems, new lenses or frameworks for viewing their worlds, new attitudes and values and even become aware of new problems. An appreciation of the value of discussion and social interaction grows out of theories of learning and can be seen in many models of teaching (Joyce and Weil, 1992) such as group investigation, inquiry training, values clarification, role-plays and simulations and those which promote cooperative learning.

In most instances, research evidence to support these commitments to various approaches to promoting interaction is either quite slender or non-existent. That does not represent, of course, grounds for abandoning them. Approaches which involve cooperative learning at compulsory education levels are one notable exception. Stallings and Stipek (1986) claim that 'positive effects of cooperative learning on achievement and attitudinal variables have been found in many carefully controlled studies' but add that the academic superiority of these approaches 'is not universally found' (p.749). An even more guarded conclusion was reached by Dunkin (1986) in a review of research on teaching in higher education. He concluded that 'at most, research might justify the choice of discussions rather than lectures where higher cognitive learnings and attitude change are the objectives' (p.756). It would appear that any commitment to interactive approaches would have to be based mainly on philosophical and experiential grounds because empirical evidence is often equivocal at best, or even non-existent. This generalization can probably be applied also to distance teaching.

A student view on interactions with other students

Some support for interactivity, especially between distance students and distance teachers, comes from students. On the basis of many years of research into learning at a distance in the context of Open University courses, Morgan (1993) concluded that 'structuring facilities for dialogue with a tutor or counsellor in our courses can help students to reflect on learning and to assist their development' (p.111). He added that 'the opportunity to discuss the work with a tutor (not necessarily in a face-to-face situation) was crucial for the development of confidence in how to tackle the work' (p.108). A recent survey of distance students enrolled in two subjects at an Australian university (Meredith, 1994) yielded similar evidence. Students in Meredith's study, although enjoying the flexibility offered by distance education, viewed the limited opportunities for regular interaction with their distance teacher and peers as a serious disadvantage. I suspect that other studies would provide affirmation of the student views outlined above but I have not made an extensive review of research to check this out. Certainly, many of the references used thus far recommend that distance teachers seek ways of interacting with their students.

The issue of student interaction with distance teachers, fellow students and other resource personnel has also been raised by others. For close on a decade, Evans and Nation (1987; 1989; 1993), for example, have been challenging a dominant model of distance education which is grounded in behaviourist notions of learning and draws on a factory model as a basis for the manufacture, packaging and distribution of information for learning. They are critical of educational packages based on programmed learning principles which oblige students to internalize the contents without providing opportunities for, or expecting, dialogue with anyone in order to satisfy assessment requirements. They refer to this model of distance education as 'instructional industrialism' and argue that it defines learning as mainly a process engaged in by individuals in isolation from others, rather than also as a social process. Moreover, they claim this model uses techniques which 'marginalise and dissolve the self-directedness of people's learning' (1989, p.249) and produces conformity and acceptance of the status quo. Their preferred option is a model of distance education which sustains dialogue between teachers and students, allows students to 'create their own discourses within a curriculum' (1989, p.248) and which challenges the hegemony of the instructor in the model of instructional industrialism in defining what knowledge is important.

In essence, they are arguing for the demise of a predominantly monologic model of distance education which features minimal interactivity between teacher and student and even less between student and student, and in support of a dialogic model which features a high level of student interactivity. Moreover, as they point out, the technology to effect this transition has been available for some time. Their favoured approach to distance education is referred to by Romiszowski (1995) as the conversational model or paradigm. He contrasts the conversational paradigm (which in his version features on-line construction of inputs or content by many participants) with what he calls the instructional paradigm (monologic model). In this approach, the inputs are designed and pre-prepared by the instructor who forwards these to the many students.

Implementing a conversational or dialogic model is not without its challenges. As Romiszowski points out, interactivity involving groups of distance students in discussions, as in seminars-at-a-distance, can pose difficulties because little is yet known about how to handle discussions via electronic networks. The two problems he addresses have to do with ensuring that participants who log in intermittently to discussions over long periods of time are able to maintain a coherent view of the content and structure of the discussion; and giving direction to the discussion so that it has a sense of purpose rather than losing focus and becoming rambling and dissipated. Some attempts at overcoming these problems involving the use of hypermedia, telecommunications and case study material are reported by Romiszowski.

Dialogue within distance education can take many forms. It can be initiated by both teacher and student; it can occur in dyads or large groups, in face-to-face settings, in written form or electronically; it can involve teachers, students, colleagues of students and other resource personnel. Dialogue can occur using a variety of technologies including pencils, telephones, computers and satellites and can involve the spoken or written word, pictures, maps, symbols and a host of other forms. Most distance teachers will be aware of the myriad forms, locations and devices for facilitating dialogue. The problem for distance teachers is deciding what purposes are to be served by use of a conversational or dialogic approach and the best means of fulfilling those purposes.

Invitation to Reflect

Think about your current practices related to student interactivity. The following questions might help.

- How often do you have contact with your students?
- In what ways and for what purposes?
- How often do students initiate contacts with you?
- Is this contact extensive? Limited? Why?
- How accessible are you? How do you inform your students of your availability?
- How do you react to them contacting you?

Now consider the appropriateness and effectiveness of your current practices:

- What information do you hold about the worth of your current practices in respect of student interactivity?
- Who else could you seek such data from? What validity checks could you run on these data?
- What are the strengths of your current practices and what are the areas for improvement?
- What other purposes for student interactivity could be added?
- How could these other purposes be fulfilled? Are these means practical?
- What is required for implementation?

Extending Student Interactivity: Implications for Practical Theories of Distance Teaching

Metaphors, as mentioned earlier, offer a useful way of reconceptualizing practical theories. In this case, the goal would be to restructure practical theories to accommodate higher levels of student interactivity. Two possible metaphors are examined briefly below. The first takes up Willis' (1993) suggestion that free hot lines be established so that students can readily contact distance teachers and other experts (librarians, technologists, administrators) in the education institution in order to get prompt attention for their questions, concerns and problems. This is a common provision in institutions offering distance programmes and is an acknowledgement of the need to break down the sense of isolation often experienced by distance students and which can contribute to unacceptably high attrition rates.

The distance teacher as a member of an emergency response team

The role of the distance teacher could thus be represented as a member of an emergency response team which is required to react quickly to calls for help in order to provide some of the conditions necessary for student survival in distance education. This view of the role of the distance teacher places a premium on rapidity of response, ensuring that potential users are aware of and can access the help system, provision of adequate technological and personnel support to maintain the system and the existence and effective use of appropriate referral strategies so that quick responses are possible. It also requires that the distance teacher have those interpersonal and communication skills needed for finding out the precise nature and origins of problems and concerns, offering remedial advice and reducing anxiety and apprehension in the student callers.

One of the limitations of this metaphor is that it does not place sufficient emphasis on proactivity on the part of the distance teacher who, as Willis suggests, needs to make regular and meaningful contact with students and actively to encourage students to identify and talk openly about their concerns. Perhaps this metaphor needs to be coupled with another, such as the distance teacher as 'safety patrol officer' so that the importance is not lost of monitoring students to ensure that none get into difficulties, or that, if they do, help is at hand.

Promoting student interactivity through the 'electronic student lounge'

Another metaphor relevant to promoting interactivity among distance students and also between them and distance teachers, was proposed by Phillips (1990). In this case, computer technology was used to create a conferencing facility to encourage computer science students enrolled in a distance programme at Massey University in New Zealand to 'meet' and confer with each other, to socialize and make friends and to form special interest groups. This facility was referred to as an 'electronic student lounge' and was reported by Phillips as serving to promote interaction and to reduce the loneliness of the distance learner. This metaphor serves as a reminder of the importance of creating a congenial context to facilitate meeting others and entering into dialogue with them. Once again the distance teacher would play an important facilitation role in publicizing and encouraging use of the facility, promoting an atmosphere of sharing, openness and cooperation among 'visitors to the lounge', posting messages on electronic message boards, forging links between students with common interests or problems and serving as a resource person. Hence possession of the right attributes by the distance teacher would go a long way to ensuring that strategies for promoting use of the electronic lounge were effective. In summary, this metaphor draws attention to such components of practical theories as teacher attributes, contextual factors and strategies and to the links between them. At the same time, it invites consideration of the values and beliefs which underpin the provision of such a facility. Of particular significance here would be values and beliefs relating to group work, cooperation, peer assessment and the role of discussion in learning.

Other implications for practical theories

So far in this section, metaphors have been used to trace some of the implications for practical theories of distance teaching of increasing interactivity between teachers and students and between students and students. Most of the discussion has focused on a few components of practical theories, in particular contextual factors, strategies and teacher attributes. Let us consider some of the possible implications of increasing student interactivity on just four other components.

To start with, what goals would be served by increasing student interactivity? One goal might be to increase the quality of learning through having learners share and negotiate their understandings and knowledge. Another goal might be to develop greater cooperation and skills in communication and group decision making and problem solving. A third goal was suggested by Morgan (1993): discussion among students is one way of facilitating the academic socialization of students. Academic socialization is the term Morgan uses to refer to finding out about the specific requirements of being a student in a subject. Like any visitor to a new culture, students enrolling in a new subject need to find out what the new 'cultural norms' are. How should they relate to the distance teacher? Is it acceptable to confer with others on study tasks? What does a 2000-word limit on an assignment really mean? How do you prepare for examinations? Can you write assignments in the first person? And so on. Often, as Morgan noted, because of 'the lack of a campus group, students experienced problems finding out what was required' (1993, p.109). Discussion among students and with teachers could help clarify these norms or requirements which are not easily communicated to distance learners through distance teaching materials.

Invitation to Reflect

Here are some questions as foci for reflection.

- Do you accept the dialogic model for distance education? Why or why not?
- If you do, what would your goals be for increasing student interactivity?
- Would you accept any of the goals discussed earlier? How would you justify your choice?

What states of mind will need to be induced or encouraged in distance students to help attain such goals? Somehow, students need to be convinced that the invisible support or counselling network is ready and able to help. They also need to be reassured that their queries and concerns will not be interpreted as indicating incompetence on their part. They need to develop confidence in their capacity to take control over their own learning and to be less timid about taking learning initiatives. Clearly, then, distance teachers need to establish and keep shoring up student confidence and trust in the system that has been designed to encourage greater interactivity. Moreover, it is crucial that distance students develop positive attitudes to interactivity and a willingness to engage with others, including their peers and teachers. Measures need to be adopted to ensure that their reservations about sharing tasks and concerns with others are reduced.

> **Invitation to Reflect**
>
> Some questions to think about:
> - What are your reactions to these ideas about student states?
> - Are they appropriate to the goals you identified above?
> - Are there other states which you would consider as important or more important?

What strategies can be used to induce these states? Strategies for encouraging interactivity include the integration into distance materials of learning activities and assessment tasks that require or expect dialogue with others. This dialogue can be induced or encouraged through activities involving field work, interviews, negotiating learning and assessment tasks, obtaining feedback from others, collaborative inquiry, conducting trials involving people, peer assessment, conferencing and group project work. Distance materials can also be designed to carry multiple voices and to invite learners to interact with these other voices and, in so doing, transform the materials. However, creating opportunities for interactivity is one thing; taking action to ensure that interactivity is maintained and reinforced is quite another. Hence the strategies listed above need to be supplemented by others, some of which were outlined earlier in discussion of metaphors related to student interactivity. Strategies are needed which will ensure that inquiries are responded to promptly, interactivity is rewarding and rewarded, learning contracts are negotiated and approved quickly, intra-group conflicts are resolved appropriately, and discussions are focused and purposeful.

> **Invitation to Reflect**
>
> Points for reflection:
> - What strategies would be appropriate in your distance course for promoting student interactivity and associated student states?
> - Are they appropriate to the students and content matter in your subject?
> - Can these strategies be resourced?

Finally, the paragraph prior to the last Invitation to Reflect hints at some of the basic principles on which strategies for promoting interactivity and accompanying student states rely for success. It would appear axiomatic that:

- Student-initiated inquiries be responded to promptly.
- Student-initiated inquiries be received positively at the institution and by the distance teacher.
- Student satisfaction with the response system be carefully monitored.
- Multiple methods for students to contact distance teachers and fellow students be developed.
- Reasons for promoting student interactivity be meaningful and valid.
- Clear and ethical guidelines for student interactivity be established.
- Students have ready access to information to facilitate interaction with their peers and teachers.

Invitation to Reflect

Give consideration to the following questions.

- Are these principles acceptable to you?
- Which ones would you not accept? Why?
- Which other key principles would you add?

Chapter 5

Review and revision of practical theories of distance teaching: additional issues

> **Focus of Chapter**
>
> As in Chapter 4, the focus in this chapter is on basic issues which confront distance teachers seeking to improve distance learning and teaching. The issues are outlined here, along with some suggested ways of resolving them, to stimulate the review and revision of your practical theories of distance teaching. Although the issues treated here have been selected because they are enduring and topical ones, they may be of little interest or relevance to you. Remember that the issues that you decide to address must be those which derive from your own work as a distance teacher. They must relate to practices which you consider are problematical or in need of improvement, and are therefore personally and professionally meaningful. Keep in mind, too, if you deem the issues dealt with here to be ones you wish to take up, that the responses or solutions that are offered may not be applicable or relevant to you. They could contain the kernel of an idea that you want to adapt and develop but, given the great variations in distance education contexts and practical theories, it is most unlikely that you will find that they provide a ready-made solution to your particular problem.

Issue 4: Promoting Better Learning

Background

At the outset, it should be noted that the term 'better learning' is to be interpreted broadly. It is intended to cover improved learning outcomes but also improved learning processes and so includes learning new or qualitatively better ways of thinking. The quality of student learning (and thinking) is a persistent discussion theme in education circles and has frequently surfaced, in the current decade, as an important topic in debates about national development in many countries around the globe. The talk has often focused on the goal of securing or establishing national futures and ways in which this goal might be achieved. These ways almost invariably involve references to a smarter, better educated and more change-oriented workforce, and one with a greater capacity for innovative and highly effective ways of thinking. Over the last two decades, calls to improve student learning have reverberated through parliaments, the meeting places of business people, industrialists and educators, and through a variety of media channels. The calls are made by those who see quality education as essential to securing attractive and worthwhile futures for individuals, communities and nations. The basic argument they present is that the individual and common good can best be served by having educational programmes which help students become innovative, creative, proactive, visionary thinkers, and who have at their disposal high-level cognitive skills such as thinking critically, reflection, and anticipating, finding, avoiding and solving problems.

These calls usually provoked a great deal of activity, both theoretical and practical, at all levels of education in many countries around the world. These countries can probably point to large collections of national reports, policies and legislative actions on measures to improve student thinking and learning. These measures have involved stocktakes of the outcomes and directions of national educational systems, reforms to curricula and teacher education, courses and research on thinking and the teaching of thinking, and the design and development of educational resource material to aid development of higher-order thinking.

Outline of the issue

What has all this activity achieved? Are educational programmes, and in particular distance programmes, really turning out top-flight thinkers in the various fields? Is encouragement of student learning in distance education any where near being optimally effective? Can more be done to facilitate high-level learning and thinking by distance students? These questions broadly indicate the nature of the first issue to be discussed in this chapter. There are a number of aspects of this issue which distance teachers could profitably reflect on. Here are three.

- How should you, as a distance teacher, respond to these calls to improve student learning (and thinking)?

- If, in your judgement, you should take some action to improve student learning, what kind or kinds of student learning should you be trying to promote?
- How can you assist students to accept the need for, and employ, these improved approaches to learning?

Responding to the call to improve student learning

Your response to the first of the above questions will depend very much on contextual realities such as the goals and level of the subject you teach and the course it serves, the backgrounds and abilities of your students, the level of satisfaction with the quality of your graduates, and institutional resources. Your response could also be informed by the results of an analysis of the kinds of thinking required of students in the subject you teach. One important question to consider is whether these kinds of thinking match the expectations of those with legitimate interests in the subject and the qualities of graduates of the course or courses to which your subject contributes. Apart from students, this group might also include credentialling agencies, employers of graduates and guardians of academic standards. A recent report of the Higher Education Council of Australia's National Board of Employment, Education and Training (1992) drew attention to some of the shifts in definitions of the generic skills (including cognitive skills) that universities should be seeking to develop through the courses they offer. The clear message was that there could be a better fit between the generic skills graduates acquire during their university studies and those their vocations or their employers require. The report also noted the importance of the role of employers in the education process and the need for 'a close interaction between them and the higher education institutions' (p.24).

Another important reference point in your assessment of the value of the learning and thinking skills your subject is designed to develop would be the performance of students in study tasks and assessment activities. Are students demonstrating the kinds of thinking in these tasks and activities that you expected or intended and that are considered essential and appropriate?

> ### Invitation to Reflect
>
> The question in the last sentence is a critical one. How might you go about fashioning a response to it? The following may indicate a useful direction to take:
>
> - What learning approaches and ways of thinking are you seeking to encourage in your subject? Do your students consider that they are developing these ways of learning and thinking in your subject?
> - Are these learning approaches and ways of thinking appropriate? How could you substantiate your response? Would others agree with your answer to the first question in this set?
> - Should there be changes (additions, deletions) to your list?

Student learning: is there cause for concern?

Keep in mind, as you make your assessment, that there still appears to be some concern about the quality of graduates and the current capacity of at least some educational programmes to promote high-level thinking. A report (Parliament of the Commonwealth of Australia, 1990) prepared by the Senate Standing Committee on Employment, Education and Training of the Australian Parliament concluded that, despite generally high standards, graduates of Australian universities are all too frequently not analytical and creative thinkers and 'are not sufficiently attuned to the need for "lifelong" learning' (p.viii). Another study by Moses and Trigwell (1993), involving students of engineering and computer subjects in a number of Australian universities, explored the ways these students were approaching their learning, using an adaptation of a learning approaches inventory. Their findings left no room for complacency. They concluded that, whereas

> the quality of student learning as measured by student approach to learning for the subjects in this study is similar to that found in Engineering in the UK,... students in both countries are reporting that they are adopting approaches to learning that are less likely to lead to understanding than students in humanities and social study disciplines. (p.27)

Moses and Trigwell also reported that, in some instances, both students and lecturers perceived that student outcomes fell short of expectations in terms of quality of learning and thinking.

One of the few studies to trace the thinking of distance students during actual study sessions (Marland *et al.*, 1992) provided some rather disturbing and quite unflattering insights into the thinking of a small sample of students. The 17 students in this study were enrolled in either an inservice Bachelor of Education course or an Associate Diploma of Community Welfare course. Both subjects provided text-based distance learning materials. To gain access to the actual thinking of students while studying, stimulated recall interviews were conducted with each student after each of three 30-minute study sessions. Videotapes of students during actual study sessions, conducted either in their own homes or a study centre, were used to stimulate recall of their thinking while studying.

The authors reported that student thinking during study sessions was superficial and possessed few indicators of quality. No in-depth or sustained evaluations of in-text material were conducted; linking of ideas to form ideational networks as an aid to understanding was limited in scope; metacognitive awareness was in evidence but few attempts were made to analyse, evaluate or direct thinking; and there was little evidence of summarizing, metaphorical thinking and student use of rehearsal strategies such as translating, paraphrasing or preparing content outlines or maps. All the evidence added up to a 'generally negative account of student thinking' (Marland *et al.*, 1992, p.215). Even those students who, in preliminary discussions of their study approaches, espoused an approach to learning which had all the hallmarks of high-order thinking and learning, performed well below the standards they had set for themselves. Several possible reasons were given to account for the kinds and levels of thinking reported. Reasons to do with the possible negative impact of the research setting and methodology, the quality of textual materials and study constraints were suggested, along with the possibility that students lacked knowledge of how to engage in high-order thinking and learning. Whatever the reasons, the quality of thinking reported by students during study sessions was very disappointing.

The general tenor of the above comments indicates that, in respect of the quality of student learning and thinking at tertiary level, there is still much room for improvement, a view which appears to have widespread acceptance (see, for example, Biggs, 1994; Morgan, 1995). The situation in primary and secondary schools looks to be no more positive, despite prodigious efforts to raise the quality of student thinking at those levels. In the USA at least, Onosko and Newmann (1994) report that 'research continues to document that low-level cognitive work dominates classroom life' (p.28). This assessment of student learning may seem rather glum and one-sided. It could have been relieved by a report on positive aspects of student learning, of which there are many. However, the point of this brief review was to make a case for working for even better results in the development of student thinking and learning. Irrespective of some notable achievements in the promotion of high levels of student cognition, evidence suggests that there is still plenty of room for improvement. Let there be no mistake about the message contained in this section then. The view being expressed here is that justifiable pride in student learning achievements should not distract attention from the fact that there appears to be plenty still to do.

> **Invitation to Reflect**
>
> Some matters for reflection:
>
> - Does the verdict about the need to improve student learning (and thinking), which admittedly rests on a small sample of documents, apply to your subject?
> - What data would you need to give a valid answer to the previous question?
> - Do you have that data?
> - If not, how can you obtain it and from whom?

One basis for judging quality of learning and thinking

Once you have the data on student thinking and learning, the next challenge that arises concerns the criteria against which you might judge their cognitive performances. Some of those criteria would presumably relate not just to their mastery of the content, but also to the thought processes they display or have learnt.

> Are they engaging in critical thinking to the depth or extent required?
> How thorough are their attempts to apply and evaluate ideas and theories?
> Are they showing sufficient inventiveness and flexibility?
> Do they really understand basic concepts?
> When engaged in decision making, are they generating appropriate and viable alternatives, enough data on the outcomes of those alternatives, and sufficiently rigorous criteria for judging those outcomes?
> Is the quality of their thinking meeting subject and academic expectations?

Your answers to these questions will depend on the kinds and levels of thinking you're trying to promote.

One useful benchmark for judging the quality of student thinking and learning, probably the best known one, is the notion of a deep approach to learning, a concept generated by Marton and Saljo (1976). This concept describes the way competent students go about a particular learning task. A useful way of describing a deep approach is to do so in terms of three concepts: study motives, strategies and conceptions of learning. Students who adopt a deep approach are motivated by intrinsic desires to develop a personal understanding of the content, academic and professional competence, new ways of looking at problems or events in the world, an interest in the content, and enjoyment from study. The strategies they use involve focusing on the author's intention and meaning, relating new content to their own experiences and work contexts, developing frameworks for making sense of, and assimilating, the material, and seeking a personal integration of the content. The use of these strategies involves higher-order thinking such as testing ideas conceptually or in practical situations; critical thinking; identifying and solving problems; generating ideas, questions, answers and theories; and evaluating the ideas encountered or created. The conception of learning, therefore, which underlies a deep approach is that of a process which ranges from understanding and applying ideas, through the development of new perspectives or new ways of looking at the world, to building new models and theories.

A deep approach to learning stands in stark contrast to a surface approach, also identified by Marton and Saljo (1976). Those students who adopt a surface approach are extrinsically motivated, principally by desires to satisfy assessment requirements set by others and to complete compulsory tasks in the subject. They are satisficers, prepared only to do enough to satisfy minimal requirements for a passing grade. They see learning as memorization and reproduction of content. The strategies they rely on include identifying discrete elements in the material to be learnt and committing them to memory by rote means. They do not seek to understand or apply what they're studying and show no inclination to place their own interpretations on the new material by reflecting on, or reorganizing, it.

The outcomes of a deep approach to learning usually include an in-depth understanding of content, the ability to use what has been learnt to describe, interpret, predict and theorize about events and the ability to formulate new insights and new ways of defining and approaching problems. These are usually regarded as the proper outcomes of a tertiary education. As Entwistle and Marton (1984) report, research has established a set of relationships between conceptions of learning, approaches to learning and outcomes which come close to logical inevitability. 'If learning is seen as "memorisation",... then the student inevitably perceives the task as an external imposition, and adopts a surface approach, which in turn excludes the possibility of reaching a deep level of understanding' (pp.222–3). In other words, surface conceptions of learning and surface approaches lead to surface outcomes; deep outcomes can only come about through the adoption of deep conceptions of learning and deep approaches.

It needs to be remembered that a deep approach may not always be necessary. This may be because a particular learning goal, task or activity may not require it. Many distance learning programmes would probably include some activities which require a surface approach and others which require a deep approach. What is important, therefore, is that students are able to adopt either approach as required and, better still, know when each is required. One other note of caution before we proceed. Some flexibility in the way a deep approach is construed would appear desirable. Harris (1995) notes that a commitment to deep learning as the only proper form of learning may be too closely aligned with a form of pedagogic idealism. Hence, he warns that, in conceptions of deep learning, there may not be sufficient account taken of the realities in which distance learners study and learn, and of the coping strategies they need to adopt. What this implies is that there are probably variations of the deep approach which could be recommended. In fact, a third approach to learning which requires use of some deep strategies and which is adopted by students who are strongly achievement-oriented has been described by Biggs (1987).

Promoting student learning

The last question to be considered in respect of this issue of promoting better learning is the 'how' question. What can be done if your review of student learning and thinking in your subject shows some deficiencies? A first step might be to ascertain why. Finding the answer will require considerable time because the reasons are varied and complex.

Sometimes the reasons are student-related. For example, students may:

- hold a surface conception of learning;
- be unable to go beyond a surface approach; or
- lack the necessary study skills through inexperience.

Sometimes, the reasons have to do with contextual factors. Because many distance learners hold jobs, lack of study time or onerous work commitments may force them into a compromise and cause them to adopt survival strategies or less satisfactory learning approaches. Yet other reasons may stem from the distance materials themselves. Poor performance in thinking and learning may be attributable, for example, to:

- an inordinately heavy reading load which induces a surface approach;
- unclear objectives or expectations which give rise to confusion as to the nature of study tasks; or
- learning materials which are poorly written, badly organized and fail to inspire.

Finally, the source of learning and thinking problems could be traced to poor communication between teacher and learner. These problems could stem from lack of contact or inadequate feedback.

Once the reasons for the learning and thinking problems are known, then various measures can be taken to address them. However, finding solutions is rarely an easy task because the learning problems that students present with are often complex, highly personal and unique. Problems to do with lack of time for study arising from heavy workloads or frequent absences from home could perhaps be alleviated reasonably quickly by adopting an open learning approach. It might involve relaxing start and finish dates for the subject or varying the times for submission of assignments, for example. Getting students to adopt a deep approach to study has been far more difficult. It is a challenge that has proven somewhat intractable, probably because adoption of a deep approach involves not just new strategies, more time and greater intellectual effort, but also a revamp of value and belief systems and study goals – which is difficult and time costly.

There is widespread support for the view that distance materials should make compelling reading, viewing and listening and that they should possess the qualities of good prose or good audio-visual presentations and be engaging, stimulating and thought-provoking. However, there is an even more strongly held conviction that distance materials must also find additional ways of engaging learners. Reading, viewing and listening are essential to learning but, if deep-level learning is to occur, the learner also needs to be actively involved in the review, application, testing, analysis and construction of knowledge. The time-honoured approach to getting students to reflect on the content of the material they are studying in these ways has usually involved the integration into distance materials of 'self-instructional activities'. This is the rubric Lockwood (1992) uses for terms such as in-text questions, self-assessment questions, adjunct aids and mathemagenic devices. The nature and purposes of self-instructional activities have been given extensive and thorough coverage in Lockwood's 1992 publication, along with reactions to, and research on, these devices and guidelines for their development; they will not be given further consideration here. Lockwood also makes a careful examination of three concepts, mentioned earlier in this text, which have influenced the design of self-instructional activities. These are the 'tutorial-in-print', the 'reflective action guide' and the notion of 'dialogue'. Once again, they will not be dealt with here. Readers can refer to the text by Lockwood (1992) where these concepts are fully explained.

It is clear then that designers of distance materials have a number of useful models on which to base the construction of self-instructional activities. It is also clear, as will be shown in any close scrutiny of distance learning packages, that designers invest considerable time and effort in the preparation of these activities which are planned to serve sound educational purposes. How well do self-instructional packages work in practice? It seems that the reactions of students to these activities could usually be described as lukewarm at best. From the limited amount of research evidence available, it appears that student by-passing of self-instructional activities may be a regular occurrence. According to Lockwood's (1992) survey of Open University student responses to in-text activities, some students complete them in accordance with instructions but 'many reduce the demands or degrade them; they reduce the intellectual demands of an activity thus making it simpler than intended and less time-consuming than expected' (p.108). Others dismiss the activities on a variety of grounds but not without some trepidation and misgivings. These findings are echoed in a study by Marland et al., (1990).

There are thus two problems here – a student proclivity to exercise the power of veto over attempting self-instructional activities; and the quality of student thinking when they do attempt them. The reasons for the first problem, which has given rise to considerable consternation among distance teachers, are thought to include an overfull curriculum, time constraints and an onerous assessment load. Finding a solution represents an important challenge but the focus in the rest of this section of Chapter 5 will be on the second problem, which has to do with raising the level of student thinking. What then can be done to encourage in students a deep approach to these activities where such an approach is appropriate or required?

The tentative answers provided below for your consideration are based on a number of key beliefs:

- that students need help in understanding and applying various kinds of thinking to the content they are studying;

- that it is the task of the distance teacher to articulate clearly the kinds of thinking required in a subject and to provide examples of those kinds of thinking as applied to the content of the subject; and
- that opportunities for students to receive feedback on their use of those kinds of thinking should be provided.

Invitation to Reflect

Before the tentative solution is suggested, you are invited to review the three beliefs outlined above to see if you find them acceptable. You could either begin the review now or first read the following statements which a distance educator might make as an explanation for holding those beliefs.

Statements:

1. I have found that many students, even at the postgraduate level, cannot demonstrate or provide adequate explanations of some common but high-level kinds of thinking denoted by requirements such as 'explain the meaning of...' or 'critically evaluate...'.
2. As a result, their responses to such tasks are often superficial, incomplete or otherwise inadequate, and their performance in assessment tasks is disappointing.
3. It is not helpful to provide students with mini-courses on thinking as preparation for enrolling in a subject because often the skills they learn in the mini-course are not readily transferred to the actual study tasks.

Questions to consider in your review:

- Do you share the beliefs outlined earlier? If not, why not?
- Is there any merit to the proposition that students be given instruction on ways of thinking and thinking about thinking in a subject they have elected or are required to study?
- How do students acquire high-order thinking skills? Might presentation of models of such thinking to students be helpful? Would conscious use of, and reflection on, such ways of thinking by students during study help in their acquisition?
- What beliefs do you hold in respect of developing the thinking skills of your distance education students?

An approach to facilitating deep learning

The approach to facilitating deep learning by distance students to be outlined below grows out of the beliefs outlined above. These beliefs appear to have carried little or no weight in the design of distance learning materials in the past because it is rare to find, in distance materials, definitions and illustrations of the kinds of thinking required in the subject. This seems rather odd because distance materials usually have many in-built devices for assisting students in their studies. Students are usually not left in any uncertainty about what is expected of them. They are frequently advised of the anticipated outcomes of their study via statements of objectives. To assist them meet those objectives, they are provided with numerous forms of assistance – learning materials, access to resources, study activities, feedback, formative assessment tasks, study guides, and a host of typographical devices such as headings, underlining and bold type. Yet many distance programmes stop short of providing advice on the kinds of thinking required and how to manifest those kinds of thinking in their study and assessment.

The strategy outlined here is aimed at filling that gap. It involves three elements:

1. Provision of cognitive specifications about the main kinds and levels of thinking required in the subject. These specifications should include clear explanations and illustrations of the types and levels of thinking.
2. Inclusion of cognitive guides provided by the lecturer for at least some self-instructional activities. These guides should provide actual suggestions about the cognitive processes and appropriate sequences that might be followed in order to complete an activity at a deep level. In addition, students could be requested to generate their own cognitive guides for some self-instructional activities.
3. Provision of feedback to students on their cognitive performances in the self-instructional activities and on the cognitive guides they themselves have generated. This feedback could be provided independently of student assessment. On the other hand, some of the activities could also contribute to the assessment programme. Thus the distance teacher would be required to adopt the role of a 'cognitive coach' who outlines the cognitive goals and the plans and processes for achieving those goals, and provides coaching services to students to assist their realization of those cognitive goals.

To help you assess the merits of this approach to facilitating a deep approach to study tasks by distance students, two examples of cognitive guides are provided.

A cognitive guide for developing conceptual understanding

The first example is directed at the development of conceptual understanding in students. This kind of understanding, understanding concepts, is usually a basic requirement in most subjects. Without a full understanding of those concepts which form an integral part of the substantive structure of the subject, progress towards mastery of the subject can be severely hampered. Concepts, then, are fundamental tools in subject mastery. Imagine the problems that students in a statistics subject would encounter, for example, if they did not understand basic concepts such as mean, mode, median, probability and variable. Failure to fully understand these concepts would place in jeopardy, or seriously erode, the benefits and progress of study in the subject.

Many students fail to gain a rich, multi-faceted understanding of a concept because they have not acquired the cognitive skills for doing so and for testing whether or not they have an adequate understanding. Various instructional models of concept attainment (see Joyce and Weil, 1992) are available and could be used in distance materials. These models are usually based on the work of Bruner *et al.*, (1967) which revealed the processes humans use for identifying the criterial attributes of concepts. Of course, distance materials show considerable variation in the ways they promote, or fail to promote, the development of conceptual understanding. Sometimes, a definition of a concept is provided and nothing else. Sometimes, an example or examples of the concept may be added, and/or a list of attributes and/or some practical applications of the concepts. Sometimes, students are provided with examples of the concept and required to formulate their own definition. Each context places different cognitive demands on students striving for conceptual understanding. Moreover, each student may have a different approach to the task of developing conceptual understanding. As a result, it is just not possible, or even desirable, to provide an invariable set or sequence of cognitive processes for use in developing conceptual understanding. Some of the cognitive processes that could be involved are:

(A) Analysing examples of x (the concept) to identify attributes.
(B) Identifying criterial attributes of x.
(C) Identifying functions served by x.
(D) Providing other examples of x.
(E) Formulating own definition of x and providing justification.
(F) Analysing various definitions of x to identify core elements.
(G) Comparing/contrasting core elements from (F) to find similarities and differences.
(H) Generating own list of core elements of x.
(I) Translating definition of x provided, into own words.
(J) Illustrating practical application of x.

Such a list, or one modified to suit particular circumstances in distance learning materials, could be provided in the self-instructional activity, and students advised to select those processes which suit their own approach. The list should also be accompanied by a number of alternative sequences that students might follow in order to develop and test their conceptual understanding. Here are some possibilities, though students would need to be advised that other sequences are possible, provided they satisfy criteria for a deep approach (the letters refer to specific processes in the list above):

$A \rightarrow B \rightarrow E \rightarrow D \rightarrow J$
$I \rightarrow D \rightarrow H \rightarrow J$
$F \rightarrow G \rightarrow B \rightarrow C \rightarrow E \rightarrow J$

A cognitive guide for model generation

Constructing a model to explain how to do something or how something works is also another common study task. Students may be asked to develop a model for change, for dissemination of a product, for testing the effectiveness of a process or for teaching others. The task may require introspection, interviews of experts, literature searches or field trials. The outcome of the task may take various forms – a flow chart, a diagram, a verbal report, a scale model or some combination of these. Obviously, model generation is a complex task, allowing for many different approaches and processes. Once again, as with the previous example, the cognitive guide that accompanies the self-instructional activity could list a wide variety of cognitive processes and alternative sequences to cater for different approaches to the task. A list of cognitive processes, such as the following, could be identified by means of task analysis to suit the particular context in the distance materials:

(K) Identify functions to be served by model for y (where y is the process, task or event).
(L) Identify issues or tasks to be addressed by the model.
(M) Articulate own model of y by introspection, reflecting on own action.
(N) Analyse models of y in the literature to identify common features.
(O) Compare/contrast models of y in the literature to identify significant components.
(P) Formulate generic features of models of y.
(Q) Construct prototype for outlining own model of y.
(R) Evaluate suitability of model conceptually and revise where necessary.
(S) Identify specifics of each component in own model of y.
(T) Test model in practical situation and revise where necessary.

Some alternative sequences for completing the task are as follows:

$K \to N \to O \to P \to S \to R$
$L \to Q \to S \to R \to T$
$O \to Q \to S \to T \to R$

Principles underpinning use of cognitive guides

The incorporation of cognitive guides into distance materials will require careful consideration of the principles underlying their use. Some of the matters which the principles should address include:

- *The frequency of provision of cognitive guides.* As indicated earlier, cognitive guides could be provided with activities which require those kinds of thinking identified as crucial in the subject. In addition, it might be wise to provide cognitive guides to illustrate what a particular kind of thinking involves and then require students to develop their own guides for other activities. Moving students towards independence in metacognition is clearly an important goal and warrants careful attention in the formulation of principles.

- *The degree of prescriptiveness in cognitive guides.* It is important that cognitive guides acknowledge diversity in human thinking and therefore allow students considerable flexibility in constructing their own approach to deep-level thinking. Providing a blueprint of how students should think and obliging students to adopt that model is unacceptable, both ethically and educationally. Thus, cognitive guides should suggest the kinds of processes and sequences that students might use to attain a deep level of thinking but they should not provide inflexible models that students feel constrained to adopt.
- *The provision of feedback.* Feedback on cognitive performance is essential to the development of both cognitive and metacognitive skills. It is essential if students are to develop the ability to assess their cognitive strengths and areas for improvement and to modify and improve the thinking that underpins their approach to learning and assessment tasks. Feedback can and should be provided from various sources – peers, distance teachers and colleagues – but it is also important that students develop a capacity for generating their own feedback.

Cognitive guides for other purposes

The notion of cognitive guides can readily be extended to other kinds of thinking though perhaps it has most relevance where tasks require relatively complex forms of thinking and where students have had little exposure to such tasks. In an era when so much emphasis is being placed on knowledge-getting skills and metacognitive awareness, it would probably make good sense to provide cognitive guides to novice distance learners for tasks such as the following:

- developing an overview or conceptual framework of a subject, chapter or topic;
- making a critical evaluation of an argument, proposition or project;
- learning from discussion in face-to-face groups or teleconferences;
- learning from video or film; and
- application of a theoretical idea in a practical situation.

An Approach to Facilitating Deep Learning: Implications for Practical Theories of Distance Teaching

The preceding account of an approach to facilitating deep learning by distance students focused on three components of a practical theory of distance teaching: beliefs, strategies and principles. It should also have been relatively easy to infer from this account what the goals of this approach were (for example, development of students' skills in higher-order thinking and learning and metacognitive awareness and control) and what the advocate of such an approach would value in terms of learning, cognition and metacognition. It is also rather obvious that a reflective state of mind in students would need to be fostered if goals are to be achieved. Another student state of mind that could play a key role in goal attainment is student acceptance of the need for, and relevance of, a deep learning approach.

> ## Invitation to Reflect
>
> This set of questions has been designed to get you to give further consideration to the implications for your practical theory of distance teaching of a commitment to fostering a deep learning approach in students.
>
> - Do you agree that willingness to be reflective and recognition of the value of deep learning are two key *student states of mind*? If not, why not? Are there other key states of mind?
> - What *strategies* could you use to foster these states of mind? Would it be possible or desirable to model these states of mind in the design of your distance materials through the use of dialogue? What are the reasons for your response?
> - What *cues* from students might indicate that they (1) appreciate the need for a deep approach and (2) are developing some understanding of what a deep approach means or involves?
> - What are the implications of fostering a deep approach for (1) the kind of feedback you give to students on performance in study tasks and assignments; (2) assessment criteria and rewarding students who engage in deep thinking and learning; (3) design of assessment activities; and (4) selection of learning resources (eg, should they exemplify a deep approach too)?
> - Are there any essential *attributes* that distance teachers, seeking to promote a deep learning approach by students, should possess in addition to a commitment to deep learning and knowledge of how a deep approach manifests itself in thinking and learning in their discipline areas?
> - What *contextual factors* (eg, student backgrounds and predispositions, institutional policies and practices, resources) might impinge on your strategies for promoting a deep learning approach? How can their facilitative impact be magnified and their adverse impact be reduced?
>
> When you have considered these aspects of your practical theory, check to see that there is internal consistency among the components.

Issue 5: Facilitating Student Access to the Content of Distance Materials

Imagine yourself on a space odyssey, about to descend on to a new planet, with no knowledge of the topography, vegetation, flora and fauna of that land, and charged with the responsibility of exploring and mapping it and finding your way across and within it. That would be a daunting task. Yet, in many respects, that is similar to the task that confronts the distance learner who enrols in a new subject and is expected to explore and gain mastery of it. They have to find out about the substance and structure of the subject, the main issues it addresses, the paradigmatic lenses through which those issues are viewed, the modes of inquiry, the conventions which shape discourse on the topic, the matters currently being contested within the subject, and a host of other matters. That, too, is a daunting task. It represents, for distance learners, a challenge which Hartley (1995) suspects is a particularly acute one.

The challenge

The challenge for the distance teacher is how to assist the new 'explorers' find their way about the new 'continent of knowledge' so that they don't become lost or mired in conceptual swamps and abort their mission. What can be done to enable distance learners to find their way about the new subject and fulfil their own expectations and those who are overseeing their journey of exploration? Clearly, their exploration of the subject would be greatly assisted if they had, to take the space explorer analogy further, the equivalent of maps, charts and photographs from space of the new planet and landing sites and possible exploration routes.

A response

One way of meeting this challenge is through the provision of access structures (Waller, 1979) in distance materials. An access structure consists of a range of devices which provide distance learners with different starting points for accessing the material to be studied and with different routes through the material. These devices include tables of contents, objectives, indices, glossaries, in-text questions, headings of various sizes, chapter titles, summaries, diagrams of the text structure and typographical cues such as using bold type to indicate significance (Hartley, 1995). Although these devices have been developed in response to the needs of readers and students of print-based materials, they are just as necessary in the preparation of other materials such as audiotapes, videotapes and CD-ROM products.

The notion of an access structure was developed by Waller in recognition of selectivity in students' reading habits. Normally, students do not proceed through textual materials in a linear fashion from start to finish. They have different needs, different interests and different knowledge backgrounds and so select what is of interest to them personally and begin reading (or viewing) where the need or interest takes them. The good thing about providing an access structure in learning materials is that it accommodates these different needs, interests and backgrounds of students and allows them to find their own ways through the material. They are not bound by a single entry point and a single pathway; they have multiple entry points and a multiplicity of pathways that they can follow and so can chart their own ways through the materials.

Research on access structures

A very useful summary of research and recommendations on the use of access devices in instructional text has been prepared by Hartley (1985) and recently updated (Hartley, 1994). The research reported by Hartley has had a diversity of foci, with some studies examining the effects of access devices on student learning and some directed at finding which layout or design of the device has the most appeal to users or works best. Very little research has been conducted into how students actually make use of the devices in natural reading or study settings. Overall, the research database is very limited in extent and very patchy, with Hartley reporting that he was unable to find any research at all in a number of areas. The research that Hartley (1985) does review, most of it conducted in experimental settings, tends to give some support to the use of titles, summaries and headings as access structure devices. He claims that studies have shown that:

> Titles affect the readers' perception and interpretation of ambiguous prose but expresses the hope that 'instructional text will not be ambiguous;
>
> Summaries aid recall of text and that 'with university students the end summary seemed more efficient, but summaries in either position were equally effective with secondary level students'); and
>
> Headings aided search, recall and retrieval but that the position and the kinds of headings used had no significant effects with the texts (that were used). (Hartley, 1985, pp.49–50)

General support for access structure devices also came from a study by Parer (1988) involving 12 tertiary-level students, six in each of sociology and modern European history. This project sought to monitor the time spent by each student and the pattern of activity on each page they were studying in a 45-minute study session using a study protocol recorder linked to a computer. Participants were also asked to complete a study approach inventory and a study process questionnaire and were then interviewed about their study methods and interactions with the textual material. Parer concluded:

> It was found that students valued and were aided by access structures… [and that] they did mention the assistance given by tables of contents, objectives, headings, introductory chapters, selective sampling and summarising. (p.87)

Finally, some interesting insights into student use of access structure features were revealed in a study which traced the moment-by-moment thinking of 17 tertiary distance students during a series of actual study sessions (Marland *et al.*, 1990). This study involved the use of videotapes of students in study sessions to stimulate recall of their thinking while studying and of the in-text features which prompted their thinking. Nine of the students were enrolled in a BEd degree while the remaining eight were enrolled in an Associate Diploma of Community Welfare (ADCW).

The study showed that there were wide variations in student use of access structure components, a few students attending to many, some students to a few and a small number not attending to any. Those most frequently attended to by BEd students were objectives, the 'how-to-study' guide and the table of contents. Headings, underlined words, summaries and in-text activities stimulated thought in only up to one-third of this group. Access devices received very little attention from the ADCW group, and then only by a half of this group. The researchers concluded that:

> provision of an elaborate access structure should be persisted with (presumably to cater for a variety of student needs and preferences), but [that] reasons for including access structure features in text should be made explicit and suggestions provided as to how they can be used by students as aids to learning. (Marland *et al.*, 1990, p.89)

Recomendations were also made in respect of other access structure components including in-text study activities.

In summary, research on access structure devices provides few categorical answers to many of the design questions of distance teachers. The findings from this research do illuminate some of the problems and ways of resolving them but, in the end, decisions about the use of access devices will have to be made by distance teachers after careful reflection on the topic and action research studies.

Implications of Access Devices for Practical Theories of Distance Teaching

The distance materials you have prepared probably already incorporate a range of access devices so that it is unlikely that your practical theory of distance teaching will have to undergo major revision to accommodate changes to your perspective on access devices. Some fine-tuning of your practical theory may be necessary where new access devices are employed or where the purposes they serve have undergone revision.

Discussion on access devices has pointed to them serving one main goal, that of providing students with many different ways of traversing the content of the subject and from many different starting points. Remember, too, that access devices can serve other purposes alluded to in the introduction to this section. For example, chapter titles, tables of contents and headings can be used to denote the scope and boundaries of the subject as well as the major topics, themes or issues that structure and comprise the content. Typographical cues such as underlining and bold type can be used to signify some of the key concepts or significant ideas to be dealt with. It might be wise to begin the review of your practical theory by defining the goals you wish to achieve through the use of access devices. Of course, goals will need to be related to contextual factors such as the level of the course, the degree of student sophistication and the nature of the subject.

Decisions will also need to be taken about the access devices or strategies that will best realize the goals that have been formulated and that are appropriate to the given context. Consideration could also be given to identifying the student states seen as desirable and then the strategies that would help to induce those states. For example, one of the recommendations from a research study cited above implied that it would be beneficial for students to have a heightened awareness of the purposes served by various access devices. Marland *et al.* (1990) reported that self-report protocols from students contained evidence that they were uncertain why words in the text were underlined. This prompted the suggestion that a strategy of making explicit the reasons for underlining words should be adopted so that students would be better able to derive the intended benefit. A similar suggestion, but in respect of headings, was made by Rowntree: 'If you suspect your learners might not otherwise be able to make good use of your headings, perhaps you'll think it worth explaining your system in the "introduction" to your lesson' (1986, p.170).

Principles on which the strategies might be based will also require careful attention. Some matters that might need to be addressed include: frequency of use of access devices; location of access devices; the format or design of access devices; and the need for a variety of access devices. It would not be difficult to overuse some devices like headings or underlining or to employ some devices which are difficult to use or understand. Excessive underlining could, for example, cause students to feel overwhelmed; an inappropriate design of an access device could induce so much confusion and frustration in students that they decline or refuse to use it. Such circumstances could incline students more towards bypassing self-instructional activities, a regrettable tendency commented on earlier.

A commitment to the use of access devices is usually aligned with certain values and beliefs similar to those held by advocates of open learning. Incorporation of an elaborate access structure into distance materials could be taken as an indication that the author values diversity and independence in students. It is an acknowledgement that distance students have a diversity of needs, interests and backgrounds, that these differences will be reflected in the ways that they interact with the materials, and that students will exercise, and should be encouraged to exercise, their independence.

> ### Invitation to Reflect
>
> Some of the implications for practical theories of distance teaching of a conscious and thoughtful use of access structure devices have been outlined above. Those implications have related to all but two of the components of practical theories.
>
> Re-read the section on implications, jotting down those that relate to: goals, values and beliefs; strategies; student states; strategies; and contextual factors. Now consider them carefully.
>
> - Are they acceptable to you? Which ones would you delete? Add? Give reasons.
> - Can you accommodate your revised list of goals, beliefs, values, etc within your practical theory of distance teaching?
> - Are there any teacher attributes which you would need to develop or refine which would increase the effectiveness of the access devices or strategies you have selected to use?

Concluding Remarks

What has been attempted over the last two chapters is to illustrate how distance teachers can change the way they teach by changing the practical theories on which their distance teaching practices are based. Five different issues have been examined, along with responses to those issues as well as what adoption of those responses would mean for the way we think about and practice our profession. Essentially, the changes we have been discussing, the changes to practical theories, require teachers to change themselves – their fundamental values and beliefs, their perspectives on teaching and learning, their prized and time-honoured ways of doing things and their views of themselves and students.

As Diamond (1991) observes, 'people change things through changing themselves first and they accomplish their concerns, if at all, only by paying the price of altering themselves' (p.120). Changing the way we teach, then, requires us to remake or transform the teacher in ourselves. As we have seen, it is a difficult, painful, time-consuming process but there is no other satisfactory way. However, it has ample rewards both in terms of our own enlightenment and in the benefits for those we teach.

References

Anning, A (1988) 'Teachers' theories about children's learning', in Calderhead, J (ed.), *Teachers' Professional Learning*, Falmer Press, London, pp.128– 45.
Batten, M, Marland, P W and Khamis, M (1993) *Knowing How to Teach Well: Teachers Reflect on Their Classroom Practice,* Research Monograph No. 44, Australian Council for Educational Research, Melbourne.
Bennett, N (1976) *Teaching Styles and Pupil Progress,* Harvard University Press, Cambridge, MA.
Berliner, D C (1986) 'In pursuit of the expert pedagogue', *Educational Researcher*, **15**, 7, 5–13.
Biggs, J (1987) *Student Approaches to Learning and Studying,* Australian Council for Educational Research, Melbourne.
Biggs, J (1994) 'Student learning research and theory: Where do we stand?', in Gibbs, G (ed.) *Improving Student Learning: Theory and Practice*, Oxford Centre for Staff Development, Oxford.
Bosworth, D P (1991) *Open Learning*, Cassell, London.
Brickhouse, N W (1990) 'Teachers' beliefs about the nature of science and their relationship to classroom practice', *Journal of Teacher Education,* **41**, 3, 53–62.
Brookfield, S D (1991) *Developing Critical Thinkers,* Jossey-Bass, San Francisco, CA.
Brookfield, S D (1995) *Becoming a Critically Reflective Teacher*, Jossey-Bass, San Francisco, CA.
Brown, S and McIntyre, D (1988) 'The professional craft knowledge of teachers', *Scottish Educational Review*, Special Issue, 39–45.
Brown, S and McIntyre, D (1993) *Making Sense of Teaching*, Open University Press, Buckingham.
Bruner, J, Goodnow, J and Austin, G (1967) *A Study of Thinking*, Science Editions, New York.
Bussis, A M, Chittenden, F and Amarel, M (1976) *Beyond Surface Curriculum,* Westview Press, Boulder, CA.
But, R, Raymond, D and Yamagishi, L (1988) 'Autobiographic praxis: Studying the formation of teachers' knowledge', *Journal of Curriculum Theorizing*, **7**, 4, 87–164.
Calderhead, J (1983) 'Research into teachers' and student teachers' cognitions. Exploring the nature of classroom teaching practice', paper presented to the annual meeting of the American Educational Research Association, Montreal.
Calderhead, J (1989) 'Reflective teaching and teacher education', *Teaching and Teacher*

Education, **5**, 43–51.

Calderhead, J (1996) 'Teachers: Beliefs and knowledge', in Berliner, D C and Calfee, R C (eds) *Handbook of Educational Psychology,* Simon and Shuster Macmillan, New York, pp.709–25.

Calderhead, J and Robson, M (1991) 'Images of teaching: Student teachers' early conceptions of classroom practice', *Teaching and Teacher Education,* **7**, 1, 1–8.

Carr, W and Kemmis, S (1983) *Becoming Critical: Knowing through Action Research,* Deakin University Press, Victoria, Australia.

Clandinin, D J (1986) *Classroom Practice: Teacher Images in Action,* Falmer Press, London.

Clark, C M (1988) 'Asking the right questions about teacher preparation: Contributions of research on teacher thinking', *Educational Researcher,* **17**, March, 5–12.

Clark, C M and Peterson, P L (1986) 'Teachers' thought processes', in Wittrock, M C (ed.) *Handbook of Research on Teaching,* 3rd edn, Macmillan, New York, pp.255–96.

Clarke, A (1995) 'Professional development in practicum settings: Reflective practice under scrutiny', *Teaching and Teacher Education,* **11**, 3, 243–62.

Connelly, F M and Clandinin, D J (1988) *Teachers as Curriculum Planners,* Teachers College Press, New York.

Cooper, P and McIntyre, D (1996) *Effective Teaching and Learning: Teachers' and Students' Perspectives,* Open University Press, Buckingham.

Copeland, W D, Birmingham, C, de la Cruz, E and Lewin, B (1993) 'The reflective practitioner in teaching: Toward a research agenda', *Teaching and Teacher Education,* **9**, 4, 347–60.

Cunningham, J B (1993) *Action Research and Organizational Development,* Praeger, Westport, CT.

Diamond, C T P (1991) *Teacher Education as Transformation,* Open University Press, Milton Keynes.

Dill, D D and Associates (1990) *What Teachers Need to Know,* Jossey-Bass, San Francisco, CA.

Donmoyer, R (1996) 'The concept of a knowledge base', in Murray, F B (ed.) *The Teacher Educator's Handbook: Building a Knowledge Base for the Preparation of Teachers,* Jossey-Bass, San Francisco, CA, pp.92–119.

Dunkin, M (1986) 'Research on teaching in higher education', in Wittrock, M C (ed.) *Handbook of Research on Teaching,* 3rd edn, Macmillan, New York, pp.754–77.

Dunkin, M and Biddle, B (1974) *The Study of Teaching,* Holt, Rinehart and Winston, Sydney.

Elbaz, F (1983) *Teacher Thinking: A Study of Practical Knowledge,* Nicholls, New York.

Elbaz, F (1988) 'Critical reflections on teaching: Insights from Freire', *Journal of Education for Teaching,* **14**, 171–81.

Elbaz, F (1991) 'Research on teachers' knowledge: The evolution of a discourse', *Journal of Curriculum Studies,* **23**, 1, 1–19.

Entwistle, N and Marton, F (1984) 'Changing conceptions of learning and research', in Marton, F, Hounsell, D and Entwistle, N (eds) *The Experience of Learning,* Scottish Academic Press, Edinburgh, pp.211–36.

Evans, T and Nation, D (1987) 'Which future for distance education?', *International Council for Distance Education, Bulletin,* **14**, 48–53.

Evans, T and Nation, D (eds) (1989) *Critical Reflections on Distance Education,* Falmer Press, London.

Evans, T and Nation, D (eds) (1993) *Reforming Open and Distance Education,* St. Martin's Press, New York.

Feiman-Nemser, S and Floden, R (1986) 'The cultures of teaching', in Wittrock, M C (ed.) *Handbook of Research on Teaching,* 3rd edn, Macmillan, New York, pp.505–26.

Fernandez-Balboa, J-M and Stiehl, J (1995) 'The generic nature of pedagogical content knowledge', *Teaching and Teacher Education*, **11**, 3, 293–306.

Foks, J (1988) *Open Learning in the State Training System*, Victorian Ministry of Education, Melbourne.

Francis, D I (1995) 'The reflective journal: A window to preservice teachers' practical knowledge', *Teaching and Teacher Education*, **11**, 3, 229–41.

Gage, N L (1978) *The Scientific Basis of the Art of Teaching*, Teachers College Press, New York.

George, R (1995) 'Open and distance learning as social practice', *Distance Education*, **16**, 1, 24–42.

Giaconia, R M (1987) 'Open versus formal methods', in Dunkin, M J (ed.) *International Encyclopedia of Teaching and Teacher Education*, Pergamon, Oxford, pp.246–57.

Gitlin, A and Teitelbaum, K (1983) 'Linking theory and practice: The use of ethnographic methodology by prospective teachers', *Journal of Education for Teaching*, **9**, 225–34.

Gore, J M and Zeichner, K M (1991) 'Action research and reflective teaching in preservice teacher education: A case study from the United States', *Teaching and Teacher Education*, 7, 2, 119–38.

Grimmett, P and Erickson, G (eds) (1988) *Reflection in Teacher Education*, Teachers College Press, New York.

Grimmett, P, MacKinnon, A, Erickson, G and Riecken, T (1990) 'Reflective practice in teacher education', in Clift, R, Houston, W and Pugach, M (eds) *Encouraging Reflective Practice in Education*, Teachers College Press, New York, pp.20–38.

Grossman, P L (1988) 'A study in contrast: Sources of pedagogical content knowledge for secondary English', unpublished doctoral dissertation, Stanford University, Stanford, CA.

Grossman, P L (1990) *The Making of a Teacher: Teacher Knowledge and Teacher Education*, Teachers College Press, New York.

Grossman, P L (1995) 'Teachers' knowledge', in Anderson L W (ed.) *International Encyclopedia of Teaching and Teacher Education*, 2nd edn, Pergamon Press, Oxford, pp.20–24.

Grundy, S and Kemmis, S (1988) 'Educational action research in Australia: The state of the art (an overview)', in Kemmis, S and McTaggart, R (eds) *The Action Research Reader*, 3rd edn, Deakin University Press, Geelong, pp.321–36.

Gudmonsdottir, S and Shulman, L (1987) 'Pedagogical content knowledge in social studies', *Scandinavian Journal of Educational Research*, **31**, 2, 59–70.

Handal, G and Lauvas, P (1987) *Promoting Reflective Teaching: Supervision in Practice*, SRHE and Open University Educational Enterprises, Milton Keynes.

Hargreaves, A (1996) 'Revisiting voice', *Educational Researcher*, **25**, January, 12–19.

Harris, D (1995) 'Still seeking the audience?', in Lockwood, F (ed.) *Open and Distance Learning Today*, Routledge, London, pp.76–84.

Harrison, N (1991) *How to Design Effective Text-Based Open Learning*, McGraw-Hill, New York.

Hartley, J (1985) *Designing Instructional Text*, 2nd edn, Kogan Page, London.

Hartley, J (1994) *Designing Instructional Text*, 3rd edn, Kogan Page, London.

Hartley, J (1995) 'The layout and design of textual materials for distance learning', in Lockwood, F (ed.) *Open and Distance Learning Today*, Routledge, London, pp.279–87.

Higher Education Council of the National Board of Employment, Education and Training (1992) *Higher Education: Achieving Quality*, Australian Government Publishing Service, Canberra.

Horwitz, R A (1979) 'Psychological effects of the "Open Classroom"', *Review of Educational Research*, **49**, 1, 71–86.

Jackson, P W (1968) *Life in Classrooms*, Holt, Rinehart and Winston, New York.

Janesick, V (1977) 'An ethnographic study of a teacher's classroom perspective', unpublished PhD thesis, Michigan State University, East Lansing, MI.

Johnson, R (1990) *Open Learning: Policy and Practice*, Commissioned Report No. 4, Australian Government Publishing Service, Canberra.

Johnson, S (1992) 'Images: A way of understanding the practical knowledge of student teachers', *Teaching and Teacher Education*, **8**, 2, 123–36.

Joyce, B and Weil, M (1992) *Models of Teaching*, 4th edn, Allyn and Bacon, Boston, MA.

Kagan, D and Tippins, D (1991) 'How student teachers describe their pupils', *Teaching and Teacher Education*, **7**, 5/6, 455–66.

Kaplan, A (1964) *The Conduct of Inquiry: Methodology for Behavioural Science*, Chandler, San Francisco, CA.

Kelly, G A (1955) *The Psychology of Personal Constructs*, Harper & Row, London.

Kemmis, S and McTaggart, R (eds) (1988) *The Action Research Planner*, 3rd edn, Deakin University, Geelong.

Lakoff, G and Johnson, M (1980) *Metaphors We Live By*, University of Chicago Press, Chicago, IL.

Lampert, M (1985) 'How do teachers manage to teach? Perspectives on problems in practice', *Harvard Educational Review*, **55**, 178–94.

Lewis, R (1995) 'Open and distance learning in Europe: Add-on or mainstream', *Open Learning*, **10**, 3, 52–6.

Lockwood, F (1992) *Activities in Self-Instructional Text*, Kogan Page, London.

Lockwood, F (ed.) (1995) *Open and Distance Learning Today*, Routledge, London.

Marks, R (1990) 'Pedagogical content knowledge: From a mathematical case to a modified conception', *Journal of Teacher Education*, **41**, 3, 3–11.

Marland, P W (1986) 'Models of teachers' interactive thinking', *The Elementary School Journal*, **87**, 2, 209–26.

Marland, P W (1993) 'A review of the literature on implications of teacher thinking research for preservice teacher education', *South Pacific Journal of Teacher Education*, **21**, 1, 51–63.

Marland, P W (1994) 'Secondary teachers' practical knowledge and conceptions of effective teaching in mathematics and science classrooms', paper presented to the annual conference of the Australian Association for Research in Education, Newcastle, New South Wales.

Marland, P W (1995) 'Implicit theories of teaching', in Anderson, L W (ed.) *International Encyclopedia of Teaching and Teacher Education*, 2nd edn, Pergamon Press, Oxford, pp.131–6.

Marland, P W and Edwards, J (1986) 'Students' in-class thinking', *Instructional Science*, **15**, 75–88.

Marland, P W and Osborne, B (1990) 'Classroom theory, thinking and practice', *Teaching and Teacher Education*, 6, 1, 93–109.

Marland, P W and Store, R (1993) 'Some instructional strategies for improved learning from distance teaching materials', in Harry, K, John, M and Keegan, D (eds) *Distance Education: New Perspectives*, Routledge, London, pp.137–56.

Marland, P W, Patching, W and Putt, I (1992) 'Thinking while studying: A process tracing study of distance learners', *Distance Education*, **13**, 2, 193–217.

Marland, P W, Patching, W, Putt, I and Putt, R (1990) 'Distance learners' interactions with text while studying', *Distance Education*, **11**, 1, 71–91.

Marland, P W, Gibson, I, Gibson, K, King, S, Lester, N and Young, P (1994) 'Effective multi-grade teaching: An exploratory study', in Marland P W and Smith K (eds) *Knowledge and Competence for Beginning Teaching. Report of a Policy Initiative*, Board of Teacher Registration (Queensland), Brisbane, pp.167–201.

Marshall, H (1990) 'Metaphor as an instructional tool in encouraging student teacher reflection', *Theory into Practice*, **xxix**, 2, 128–32.

Marton, F and Saljo, R (1976) 'On qualitative differences, outcomes and process I and II', *British Journal of Educational Psychology*, **46**, 4–11 and 115–27.

Maxwell, L (1995) 'Integrating open learning and distance education', *Educational Technology*, 35, 6, 43–8.

Mayer, D, Cornford, L, Marland, P W, Olsen, P and Phillips, S (1994) 'Teachers' knowledge of students: A significant domain of practical knowledge?', in Marland, P W and Smith, K (eds) *Knowledge and Competence for Beginning Teaching. Report of a Policy Initiative*, Board of Teacher Registration (Queensland), Brisbane, pp.167–201.

Meredith, N S (1994) 'Whither the learner in distance teaching and learning', unpublished MEd Studies thesis, University of Queensland, Brisbane.

Morgan, A (1993) *Improving Your Students' Learning*, Kogan Page, London.

Morgan, A (1995) 'Student learning and students' experiences: Research, theory and practice', in Lockwood, F (ed.) *Open and Distance Learning Today*, Routledge, London, pp.55–66.

Moses, I and Trigwell, K (1993) *Teaching Quality and Quality of Learning in Professional Courses*, Australian Government Publishing Service, Canberra.

Munby, H and Russell, T (1989) 'Metaphor in the study of teachers' professional knowledge', paper presented at the annual meeting of the American Educational Research Association, San Francisco, CA.

Oliver, R and Grant, M (1994) *Distance Education Technologies: A Review of Instructional Technologies for Distance Education and Open Learning*, Edith Cowan University, Perth.

Onosko, J J and Newmann, F M (1994) 'Creating more thoughtful learning environments', in Mangieri, J and Block, C (eds) *Creating Powerful Thinking in Teachers and Students: Diverse Perspectives*, Harcourt Brace Jovanovich, New York, pp.27–49.

Parer, M (1988) *Textual Design and Student Learning*, Centre for Distance Learning, Gippsland Institute of Advanced Education, Churchill, Victoria.

Parliament of the Commonwealth of Australia (1990) *Priorities for Reform in Higher Education, A report of the Senate Standing Committee on Employment, Education and Training* (Chair: Senator T Aulich), Australian Government Publishing Service, Canberra.

Paul, R (1992) *Critical Thinking*, 2nd edn, Foundation for Critical Thinking, Santa Rosa, CA.

Phillips, C (1990) 'Making friends in the "electronic student lounge"', *Distance Education*, **11**, 2, 320–33.

Phillips, R, Watson, A and Wille, C (1993) 'Teacher knowledge and teacher behaviour in composite classes', *St. George Papers in Education*, **1**.

Ritchie, S and Russell, B (1991) 'The construction and use of a metaphor for science teaching' *Research in Science Education*, **21**, 281–99.

Romiszowski, A J (1995) 'Use of hypermedia and telecommunications for case-study discussions in distance education', in Lockwood, F (ed.) *Open and Distance Learning Today*, Routledge, London, pp.164–72.

Ross, D D (1989) 'Action research for preservice teachers: A description of why and how', *Peabody Journal of Education*, **64**, 3, 131–50.

Ross, D D (1990) 'Programmatic structures for the preparation of reflective teachers', in Clift, R, Houston, W and Pugach, M (eds) *Encouraging Reflective Practice in Education*, Teachers College Press, New York, pp.97–118.

Rowntree, D (1986) *Teaching through Self-instruction: A Practical Handbook for Course Developers*, Kogan Page, London.

Rowntree, D (1992) *Exploring Open and Distance Learning*, Kogan Page, London.

Sanders, D P and McCutcheon, G (1986) 'The development of practical theories of teaching', *Journal of Curriculum and Supervision*, **2**, 1, 50–67.

Schön, D (1983) *The Reflective Practitioner: How Professionals Think in Action*, Basic Books, New York.

Schön, D (1987) *Educating the Reflective Practitioner*, Jossey-Bass, San Francisco, CA.

Schön, D (ed.) (1991) *The Reflective Turn. Case Studies In and On Educational Practice*, Teachers College Press, New York.

Shulman, L S (1986) 'Those who understand: Knowledge growth in teaching', *Educational Researcher*, **15**, 2, 4–14.

Shulman, L S (1987) 'Knowledge and teaching: Foundations of the new reform', *Harvard Educational Review*, **57**, 1–22.

Smyth, J (1989) 'An alternative vision and an "educative" agenda for supervision as a field of study', *Journal of Curriculum and Supervision*, **4**, 2, 162–77.

Snow, R E (1973) 'Theory construction for research on teaching', in Travers, R M W (ed.) *Second Handbook of Research on Teaching*, Rand McNally, Chicago, Ill, pp.77–112.

Sockett, H (1987) 'Has Shulman got the strategy right?', *Harvard Educational Review*, **57**, 2, 208–19.

Stallings, J and Stipek, D (1986) 'Research on early childhood and elementary school teaching programs', in Wittrock, M C (ed.) *Handbook of Research on Teaching*, 3rd edn, Macmillan, New York, pp.727–53.

Stringer, E T (1996) *Action Research. A Handbook for Practitioners*, Sage, London.

Tabachnick, R and Zeichner, K (1991) *Issues and Practices in Inquiry-oriented Teacher Education*, Falmer Press, London.

Thorpe, M and Grugeon, D (1987) 'Moving into open learning', in Thorpe, M and Grugeon, D (eds) *Open Learning for Adults*, Longman, Harlow.

Tiberius, R G (1986) 'Metaphors underlying the improvement of teaching and learning', *British Journal of Educational Technology*, **17**, 2, 144–56.

Tobin, K (1990) 'Changing metaphors and beliefs: A master switch for teaching', *Theory into Practice*, **xxix**, 2, 122–7.

Toffler, A (1970) *Future Shock*, Random House, New York.

Tom, A R (1988) 'Replacing pedagogical knowledge with pedagogical questions', in Smyth, W J (ed.) *Educating Teachers*, Edward Arnold, Melbourne, pp.9–17.

van Manen, M (1977) 'Linking ways of knowing with ways of being practical', *Curriculum Inquiry*, **6**, 205–28.

Wade, W and Sutton, J (eds) (1994) *Flexibility in Course Provision in Higher Education*, Annual Report, Loughborough University of Technology, Loughborough.

Walker, J (1994) 'Open learning: The answer to the government's equity problems? A report of a study in the potential impact of the open learning initiative on people with disabilities', *Distance Education*, **15**, 1, 94–111.

Waller, R (1979) 'Typographical access structures for educational texts', in Koplers, P A, Wrolstad, M E and Houma, H (eds) *Processing of Visible Language*, Vol 1, Plenum Press, New York.

West, M (1976) *The Navigators*, Collins, New York.

Willis, B (1993) *Distance Education: A Practical Guide*, Educational Technology Publications, Englewood Cliffs, NJ.

Woods, P (1987) 'Life histories and teacher knowledge', in Smyth, W J (ed.) *Educating Teachers*, Edward Arnold, Melbourne, pp.121–35.

Yaxley, B G (1991) *Developing Teachers' Theories of Teaching: A Touchstone Approach*, Falmer Press, London.

Yinger, R, Hendricks-Lee, M S and Johnson, S (1991) 'The character of working knowledge', paper presented at the annual meeting of the American Educational Research Association, Chicago, IL.

Zeichner, K M and Liston, D P (1987) 'Teaching student teachers to reflect', *Harvard Educational Review*, **57**, 23–48.

Author Index

Amarel, M 20
Anning, A 80
Austin, G 104

Batten, M 23, 24, 28, 29, 34, 39, 40
Bennett, N 30
Berliner, D C 42
Biddle, B 21, 34
Biggs, J 97, 99
Birmingham, C 53, 54, 55, 57
Bosworth, D P 69, 73
Brickhouse, N W 20
Brookfield, S D 6, 59
Brown, S 4, 7, 24, 25, 28, 34, 40
Bruner, J 104
Bussis, A M 20
But, R 13

Calderhead, J 12, 38, 58, 77
Carr, W 7
Chittenden, F 20
Clandinin, D J 9, 38, 39
Clark, C M 9, 20, 32, 61
Clarke, A 53, 54
Connelly, F M 9
Cooper, P 23, 28, 29, 40
Copeland, W 53, 54, 55, 57
Cornford, L 35, 37, 79, 80
Cunningham, J B 63

de la Cruz, E 53, 54, 55, 57
Diamond, C T P 112
Dill, D D 18
Donmoyer, R 4–5

Dunkin, M 21, 34, 85

Edwards, J 21
Elbaz, F 4, 17, 34, 42, 60, 79
Entwistle, N 99
Erickson, G 53, 56, 58
Evans, T 85–6

Feiman-Nemser, S 9
Fernandez-Balboa, J-M 43
Floden, R 9
Foks, J 69
Francis, D I 13, 54, 60–61

Gage, N L 20
George, R 71
Giaconia, R M 69, 71
Gibson, I 23
Gibson, K 23
Gitlin, A 60
Goodnow, J 104
Gore, J M 53, 55, 60
Grant, M 71
Grimmett, P 53, 56, 58
Grossman, P L 42, 43
Grugeon, D 70
Grundy, S 63
Gudmonsdottir, S 42

Handal, G 7–8, 58
Hargreaves, A 17
Harris, D 99
Harrison, N 77, 78, 81
Hartley, J 108, 109

Hendricks-Lee, M S   4
Higher Education Council (HEC)   95
Horwitz, R A   69

Jackson, P   61
Janesick, V   23
Johnson, M   61
Johnson, R   69, 70, 74
Johnson, S   4, 38
Joyce, B   28, 29, 30, 85, 104

Kagan, D   79
Kaplan, A   6
Kelly, G A   6
Kemmis, S   7, 63, 64–5
Khamis, M   23, 24, 28, 29, 34, 39, 40
King, S   23

Lakoff, G   61
Lampert, M   19
Lauvas, P   7–8, 58
Lester, N   23
Lewin, B   53, 54, 55, 57
Lewis, R   71
Liston, D P   55, 60
Lockwood, F   73, 84, 101

MacKinnon, A   53, 56
Marks, R   42, 43
Marland, P W   8, 9, 19, 21, 23, 24, 26–7, 28, 29–30, 31, 34, 35, 37, 39, 40, 44, 79, 80, 96, 97, 101, 109–10
Marshall, H   60, 61–2, 63
Marton F   98, 99
Maxwell, L   71
Mayer, D   35, 37, 79, 80
McCutcheon, G   7, 8
McIntyre, D   4, 7, 23, 24, 25, 28, 29, 34, 40
McTaggart, R   64–5
Meredith, N S   85
Morgan, A   85, 89, 97
Moses, I   96
Munby, H   36–7

Nation, D   85–6
Newman, F M   97

Oliver, R   71

Olsen, P   35, 37, 79, 80
Onosko, J J   97
Osborne, B   19, 26–7, 29, 34, 35, 40, 44

Parer, M   109
Parliament of the Commonwealth of Australia   96
Patching, W   96, 97, 101, 109–10
Paul, R   59
Peterson, P L   20, 32, 61
Phillips, C   88
Phillips, R   35, 80
Phillips, S   35, 37, 79, 80
Putt, I   96, 97, 101, 109–10
Putt, R   101, 109–10

Raymond, D   13
Riecken, T   53, 56
Ritchie, S   37, 60, 62–3
Robson, M   38
Romiszowski, A J   86
Ross, D D   58, 60
Rowntree, D   31, 73, 78, 81, 84, 111
Russell, B   37, 60, 62–3
Russell, T   36–7

Saljo, R   98, 99
Sanders, D P   7, 8
Schön, D   4, 51, 52–3, 56, 57, 58, 59, 61
Shulman, L S   42
Smyth, J   60
Snow, R E   39
Sockett, H   18, 40
Stallings, J   85
Stiehl, J   43
Stipek, D   85
Store, R   31
Stringer, E T   64
Sutton, J   71

Tabachnick, R   58
Teitelbaum, K   60
Thorpe, M   70, 105
Tiberius, R G   37, 61
Tippins, D   79
Tobin, K   37, 60, 61, 62–3
Toffler, A   37
Tom, A R   18
Trigwell, K   96

van Manen, M 54

Wade, W 71
Walker, J 71
Waller, R 108
Watson, A 35, 80
Weil, M 28, 29, 30, 85, 104
West, M 3

Wille, C 35, 80
Willis, B 87–8
Woods, P 13

Yaxley, B G 13
Young, P 23
Yinger, R 4

Zeichner, K M 53, 55, 58, 60

Subject Index

access structure 107–11
  devices in 108
  implications for practical theories 110–11
  research into effects and student use of 109–10
action research 63–5
  characteristics of 64
  Deakin model of 63–4
  definition of 64
  processes of 64–5
actions, *see* strategies
aims, *see* goals
articulation of practical theories 11–13
  difficulties in 12
  methods for 12–13
attributes, *see* teacher attributes

beliefs 18, 20–21, 22, 45, 75, 101–2, 111
  congruence with actions 20
  durability of 21
  flaws in 21
  place in practical theory of 40–41

cognitive guide 103–6
  for developing conceptual understanding 103–4
  for model generation 105
  for other purposes 106
  principles underpinning use of 105–6
conceptual understanding 103–4
contextual factors 18, 34–6, 48, 75
conversational model, *see* dialogic model
craft knowledge, *see* practical knowledge

critical thinking 58–60
  and reflection 58
  key components of 59
cues 18, 26–8, 41

dialogic model in distance education 86
  challenges in implementation 86
dialogue, *see* interactions
dilemmas 19
  management of 19

epistemology of practice 53

feedback on cognitive performance 103

goals 18, 23–4, 45, 75, 89

humans as 'personal scientists' 6–7

images 18, 38–9
  as mental coalescences of experiences 38–9
  as mental snapshots 38
  impact on teaching 39
  place in structure of practical theory 41
instructional industrialism 86
interactions 84–91
  among distance students, teachers and others 84
  distance student view on value 85
  implications for practical theories 87, 89–90
  promotion 88

rationale   84–5
   via the 'electronic student lounge'   88
   with text   84

journals   13
journal writing   60–61
   conditions for improving effectiveness   60–61
   framework for   60

knowledge colonization   17
   problems   17–18
knowledge of students   76–8
   effects of inadequacies in   76
   implications for practical theories   82–3
   means for acquisition   79, 81
   required for course design   77–8
   required for teaching   79, 81
   value of   80

learning (and thinking) of students   94–107
   assessing need for improvements   94–5
   deep approach   98–9
      facilitation of   102–6
      implications for practical theories   106–7
   importance of   94
   quality of   96
   reasons for deficiencies   100
   shifts in generic skills   95
   surface approach   99

metaphors   18, 36–8, 40, 61–3, 88
   as a way of reconceptualizing teaching   61–3
   as a way of representing reality   61
   as 'master switches'   61–2
   distance teacher as a member of an 'emergency response team'   88
   in distance teaching   38, 88
   of teachers   37
   place in practical theories   40–41
   teacher as 'travel agent'   37, 62
methods, *see* strategies
models of teaching, *see* strategies
mood assessment   26, 35

normal desirable states, *see* student states

open education   68–9
open learning   68
   implications for practical theories   72–5
   meaning   69
   reasons for advocacy   69–71
   research   71–2
   trend towards   68

pedagogical content knowledge (PCK)   18, 42–4
   components   42
   example   43
   meaning   42–3
performance, *see* strategies
practical know-how, *see* practical knowledge
practical knowledge   1–2, 4
   categories, domains   42
   characteristics   5–6
   examples   2–4
   links with research/scientific knowledge   4
   sources   4
practical theories   6–48
   and scientific theories   8
   articulation of   11–13
   as basis for review of teaching   11
   characteristics   8
   concepts for representing substance   18
   definition   7–8
   example in distance teaching   44–8
   functions   8
   impact on teaching   9
   implications for teachers, distance teachers   9–11
   model of structure   40–41
   of student teachers   7
   of teachers   7–8
   review, revision   51
   significance   8–9
   structure   39–41
   substance   17–39
principles   18, 32–3, 47, 75, 89, 105–6, 111
   suppressing emotions   32
   strategic leniency   32

reflection, reflective practice   53–60
   and critical thinking   58

as distinct from technical problem
      solving   53–4
   definition   57–8
   example   56–7
   kinds   54
   levels of technical, practical, critical
      54–5
   processes   56
   promotion   60
   use of research knowledge   56

scientific knowledge   2
   use in professional practice   4
self-instructional activities   101
   student power of veto over   101
   student reactions   101
student interactivity, *see* interactions
student states   18, 24–6, 28, 41, 46–7, 75, 89, 111
strategies   18, 28–32, 46, 73, 75, 89

   for encouraging a deep approach
      102–6
   functions of   30
   in distance education   30–31

tacit knowledge   4
tactics, *see* strategies
teachable moment   26
teacher attributes   18, 33–4, 41, 47, 75
teacher knowledge categories   42
teacher voice   17
teachers as theory builders   7
theorizing tendency in people   6
tutorial-in-print   31, 84, 101

values   18–20, 22, 40–41, 45, 75, 111
   place in structure of practical theories   41

working knowledge, *see* practical knowledge

Open and Distance Learning Series

Series Editor: Fred Lockwood

Activities in Self-Instructional Texts, Fred Lockwood
Exploring Open and Distance Learning, Derek Rowntree
Improving Your Students' Learning, Alistair Morgan
Key Terms and Issues in Open and Distance Learning, Barbara Hodgson
Managing Open Systems, Richard Freeman
Mega-Universities and Knowledge Media, John S Daniel
Objectives, Competencies and Learning Outcomes: Developing Instructional Materials in Open and Distance Learning, Reginald F Melton
Open and Distance Learning: Case Studies from Industry and Education, Stephen Brown
Open and Flexible Learning in Vocational Education and Training, Judith Calder and Ann McCollum
Preparing Materials for Open, Distance and Flexible Learning, Derek Rowntree
Programme Evaluation and Quality, Judith Calder
Teaching Through Projects, Jane Henry
Teaching with Audio in Open and Distance Learning, Derek Rowntree
The Costs and Economics of Open and Distance Learning, Greville Rumble
Towards More Effective Open and Distance Teaching, Perc Marland
Understanding Learners in Open and Distance Education, Terry Evans
Using Communications Media in Open and Flexible Learning, Robin Mason